JAPANESE DECORATIVE ARTS

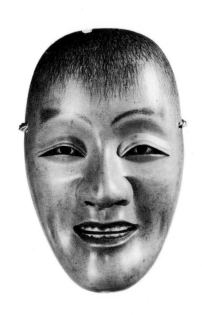

JAPANESE

Lawrence Smith
and Victor Harris

DECORATIVE ARTS
from the 17th to the 19th centuries

BMP

Published for the
Trustees of the British Museum by
British Museum Publications Limited

Published by British Museum Publications Ltd,
46 Bloomsbury Street, London WC1B 3QQ

Smith, Lawrence,
    Japanese decorative arts from the 17th to the 19th centuries.
    1. Art, Decorative—Japan—History
    I. Title   II. Harris, Victor
    745′.0952   NK1484

    ISBN 0–7141–1421–9

Designed by Harry Green

Set in Monophoto Photina
and printed in Great Britain by
Jolly & Barber Ltd, Rugby.

Page 1 Mask of a *shōjō* for the *Nō* drama,
signed Munetada. Painted wood.
18th century. H. 20.8 cm. (See also p. 61.)

Pages 2–3 Sword blade with two grooves.
Hamon of 'wild' *nie*. Signed 'Made by Fujiwara
Kunisada resident in Mushū province'.
Horikawa school, early 17th century.
L. excluding tang 71.3 cm. (See also p. 37.)

Opposite Detail of a chantress from the
woodblock book *Ryakuga Shokunin Zukushi*
by Gakutei, 1826. Each leaf 220 × 135 mm.

CONTENTS

Preface   6

1   Introduction   8

2   Metalwork   24

3   Sculpture and
    decorative carving   52

4   Lacquer   76

5   Ceramics   104

6   Postscript – textiles
    and the hidden
    artefacts of Japan   122

Bibliography   126

Japanese
historical periods   127

Index of
Japanese terms   127

PREFACE

The British Museum houses a large and fine collection of the applied or decorative arts of Japan from the period 1600 to 1900. It is especially comprehensive in four areas of traditional collecting in Europe – swords and sword-fittings; lacquer, in particular *inrō*; small-scale carving, notably netsuke; and ceramics. Indeed, the Museum owes its rich holdings very largely to those enthusiastic collectors of the last 125 years who gave or bequeathed their collections to the nation. Of these the most recent was the late Captain Collingwood Ingram, who died in 1981 aged 100, to whose memory we most affectionately dedicate this book. A number of his pieces are illustrated.

The existence of keen collectors in the above-mentioned fields of Japanese decorative art has led to the existence of a wide literature about them in English and other European languages. It must be said, and this is in no way to criticise these works, that they are all extremely specialised; in them can be found those extensive lists of makers and detailed descriptions of techniques and Japanese technical terms that the enthusiast requires. A selection of them is listed in the Bibliography. This book attempts to do something different – to place those arts in their wider context of Japanese traditional material culture and to show how they fit into it.

Victor Harris has been responsible for the chapters on lacquer and metalwork; the others are by myself. We are grateful to Joe Cribb of the Department of Coins and Medals for writing the section on Japanese coinage. We should also like to thank David Gowers of the British Museum Photographic Service for his excellent photographs, and our many colleagues in the Department of Oriental Antiquities who have helped us, especially Greg Irvine who has always been ready with practical assistance.

LAWRENCE SMITH *Keeper of Oriental Antiquities*

1. Detail of a fan-maker from *Saiga Shokunin Burui* by Minkō, 1770. Each leaf 285 × 190 mm.

1 INTRODUCTION

2. Street outside the Iwaki drapery store in Edo. A triptych woodblock print by Hiroshige. *c.* 1850. Each sheet 370 × 250 mm.

The term 'decorative arts' has been chosen to embrace the varied objects which are the subject of this book. It is not, however, a fully appropriate term, because the Japanese have not in their traditional culture divided things decorated from things undecorated, and there have not been readily available words in the Japanese language to describe that distinction. Instead, they have placed value on both the visual and sensuous impact of an object taken as a whole, be it at one extreme plain pottery or bamboo, or at the other elaborately adorned lacquer or metalwork.

A better word, therefore, might have been 'applied arts', which in English makes the distinction from 'fine arts'. That contrast has been made in Japan itself in the last 100 years, at least since the setting up of the Tokyo Art School. The intention of that institution was partly the preservation of Japanese arts of all sorts from extinction in the face of overwhelming Western influence; about that time the words *bijutsu* (fine arts) and *kōgei* (applied arts) came to be used. *Kōgei* literally means 'skilled arts', and had to be adopted for those more obviously decorative crafts which were then in vogue and had acquired particular prestige because of demand and enthusiasm from the Western world. Small-scale ivory sculpture and cloisonné enamels were noticeable examples.

That more selective concept, however, was made in response to the impact of Western ideas and does not hold true for the period which occupies the major part of this book, during which the arts and crafts we wish to examine had no specific name of their own. Their makers, though, *did* have a name. They were included among the *shokunin* (craftsmen/artisans), who composed the third of the four official classes of society in the formal, legal divisions laid down in the seventeenth century. It is the material products of the *shokunin*, in so far as they are represented in Western collections, with which we are mainly concerned.

Nevertheless, the word *shokunin* itself was wider than the above definition implies, for it included all sorts of occupations which would not be suggested by the English word 'craftsman'. We know this from the collections of pictures known as *Shokunin zukushi*, or 'Exhaustive lists of craftsmen', which were produced from at least as early as the sixteenth century. Their popularity itself shows the deep interest the educated Japanese public took in professional technique, not only in the material crafts but also in the various forms of entertainment, extending to the *geisha* (who were professional hostesses and conversationalists).

However, painters themselves were considered *shokunin*, except for those members of the nobility and samurai classes who did not paint for money and the 'scholar artists' of the eighteenth and nineteenth centuries; so our distinction is only partly true. The fact is that the culture of Japan, at least until Western industrialisation began to affect it in the 1850s, was both complex and exceptionally integrated, and to try to divide it in Western style into higher or lower arts, prestigious or inferior skills is likely to lead to misconceptions. The cultural attitudes of the Tea Ceremony are a reflection of that total approach to environment, architecture, garden and interior design, dress, utensils and behaviour which characterises Japanese culture at its most satisfying.

Perhaps the only definition which comes near to a useful meaning is

9

that of function. Even in Japan there were things which had no function except to be looked at. Of these paintings and prints were by far the most important, and one could argue that there were no other man-made objects which had no secondary function. Among paintings, indeed, there were types which had a definite use – folding screens, standing screens, *fusuma* (sliding doors) and fan paintings are the most important – but there were others which existed only to be looked at – hanging scrolls, handscrolls and albums.

This book, then, is about objects of use made by *shokunin* during the period 1600–1900. *Shokunin* as a class ceased to exist with the social reorganisation of the early Meiji period (1868 and after), and with those upheavals came a change towards the manufacture of many types of object, supposedly decorative and often without any function, for the Western market, where the late-nineteenth-century taste for domestic clutter, especially in north-west Europe, was at its height. Western collections are full of these things; and the greater part, too, of what was brought back from the centuries before 1868 was naturally what Westerners were able to recognise from their own culture as admirable – sword blades, richly decorated sword-fittings, armour, ornate bronze vessels, clocks, fine and less fine porcelain, pottery with brilliant enamels, lacquer with much gold, miniature carvings, and painted screens and sets of doors. There was, as well, an overwhelming interest in the non-functional woodblock prints.

More space is given, therefore, to these categories than they strictly deserve, because it is they that are available outside Japan. Far less appreciated and collected were whole categories of objects which required as great or greater skill and commanded much admiration in their own country, but because of their austerity, unfamiliarity, the low prestige of their Western counterparts, or sheer fragility never gained interest. Examples of these types are the pottery and iron vessels used in the Tea Ceremony; woven bamboo baskets, carved seals and plain wooden boxes; dolls, textiles and costume; and objects made of leather or paper, including origami. These and others are mentioned, though at less length.

Their equivalents in the non-functional sphere are the less popular styles of painting and above all calligraphy, which during the Heian period (794–1185) achieved a prestige far in excess of any other visual art, which it was never entirely to lose. As a result, the crafts essential to it – writing-boxes, brushes, inkstones, ink-cakes, paper and silk, seals and seal-paste – had to achieve extremely high standards.

One of the most interesting ways of introducing traditional Japanese material culture is to consider the many types of object a Westerner would expect to find in a museum collection from his own past, which ones are also to be found in Japan, and which are missing. Then, perhaps most interesting of all, it becomes clear which artefacts are unique to Japan, or East Asia as a whole.

In the West painting, prints and sculpture have for long been considered the major arts, and many galleries are devoted exclusively to one or other of them. Museums of the arts and crafts defined as decorative will normally be dominated by furniture, including musical instruments, clocks and watches, porcelain and pottery, glass, gold, silver and pewter, jewellery, costume and textiles, firearms and swords with scabbards.

A collection of traditional Japanese arts and crafts will include a number of these. Painting, as we have seen, certainly exists but in very different materials and formats. Prints, too, at least if we begin from the late seventeenth century onwards, are found in large numbers. Sculpture also is found but nearly all of it in the Western sense is religious, and most of that is Buddhist. We shall find small furniture, such as very low tables and portable sets of shelves, small musical instruments, and a limited number of clocks. Pottery and porcelain will be as common as in a Western collection, so will arms and armour, and so would textiles and costume if more interest had been taken in them outside Japan.

This list leaves some very obvious omissions. The most noticeable are gold, silver and pewter, which hardly exist at all in their own right in Japanese culture. The same is true of jewellery, for which there was no consistent taste until the late nineteenth century. Glass was made from

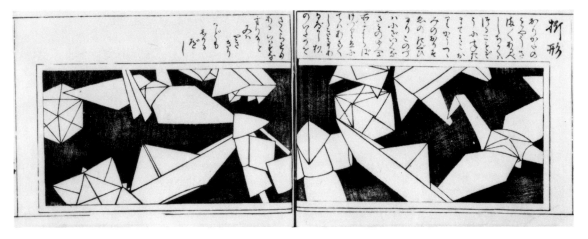

3. Origami (folded paper) models, arranged as a pattern for wooden transom panels, from the woodblock book *Ramma Zushiki* by Shumboku, 1734. 191 × 257 mm.

time to time – a moderate amount in the eighteenth and nineteenth centuries – but it never caught on and has survived only in small quantities. Oil-painting and secular, monumental and ornamental sculpture only began to be produced in the Meiji period except for isolated outbreaks approaching eccentricity; of large-scale furniture there is nothing at all.

Yet the gaps apparently left in the field of fine and decorative arts by these absences are filled by several types of object which are especially interesting either because they are not valued in other cultures as they are in Japan or because they exist only there or in the Far East. They include bronze mirrors and incense-burners, hair-combs and pins in wood and lacquer; woven and carved bamboo baskets, vases, wrist-rests and brush-jars; and miniature items of personal adornment and use, such as seal-cases, tobacco boxes, purses and writing-sets, with their acompanying toggles and slides, and the elaborate braids used to tie them; inkstones, ink-cakes and brushes; many different things made from the superb-quality hand-made papers of Japan; and dolls.

It is easiest to understand these differences by looking at the physical basis of Japanese culture in this period and the assumptions about life which lay behind it. Everything described below under this head was well established by 1600 and continued with little change until the 1850s,

4. Matsumoto Castle, showing foundations made of large stone blocks.

when Western industrialisation finally began to have a pronounced effect.

Japanese life was physically insecure – earthquakes, active volcanoes, landslips, typhoons and tidal waves made any attempt to build permanently in stone out of the question. The volcanic soil of most of the country did not produce much building stone in any case. Because some 80 per cent of the country was covered with almost unusable steep hills with a crumbling surface, building, living and agriculture had to be carried out in the remaining 20 per cent, all of which was near to the sea and subject to flood and typhoons. Buildings were therefore made very largely from timber, the one major resource of those hills, and only the foundations might use stone. This was true even of the castles which had begun to spring up in the later sixteenth century.

The necessity of living in this way led to another, perhaps even greater hazard – fire. No large building could expect to survive through the centuries without being burned down and rebuilt once or more times. In the city of Edo, where huge earthquakes periodically struck, the fires which followed did most of the damage.

Physical culture, therefore, developed to be replaceable, renewable or portable. Anything which might be rescued from a fire would have to be small and light enough to be carried easily, and it would have to be capable of being packed in a way which would protect it from heat and flames. The methods of boxing and storage which developed to meet this end also, with characteristic Japanese economy, served to protect objects from the effects of heat and damp, and from the insects which in the semi-tropical summer months play such a noticeable part in the scene.

The basic method of construction of a Japanese building did not vary, except for the castles, which were usually built on a huge substructure of dressed stone (4). These must be regarded as exceptions, whose imposing structures were at first military but later symbolic of the power of the *daimyō* or provincial overlords appointed by or at the least tolerated by the Tokugawa shoguns. The method was that of a skeleton of wooden pillars, set in or on stone bases. The floors of the building were hung round these pillars on beams, at a height of a metre or so above the ground; in that way damp and insects were kept at bay and a useful area for storage (not, of course, extending down to soil level) provided. The frontage of a building did extend down to street level, as can be seen in the print of an Edo street scene (2), but usually inside the outer door there would be a stone step up to the raised floor. Kitchen areas were often at the lower level, over a stone floor, with drainage channels which were constantly washed down with water. To protect their feet from this damp kitchen workers wore the very high, wooden clogs called *geta*, also often worn in the street.

Into the skeleton of pillars and beams the rest of the building could be fitted. The roof might consist of large pottery or wooden tiles, all easily replaceable. Only in the mountainous country areas, in the isolated valleys and plateaux where life was possible, was reed thatch used. The walls, ceilings and floors all consisted largely of detachable units, and it is this that has led to the justifiable claim that the Japanese pioneered what we now call modular architecture and interior decoration. Any permanent areas, such as wall space beneath higher-level windows, were filled in with a simple plaster over rice-straw, but even they were normally made in small modular sections which could be replaced without affecting the whole wall space. The back wall of the *tokonoma* (see p. 26) was traditionally made in that way.

Although walls and ceilings might seem at first more important, it was in fact the floors of Japanese buildings that had the biggest influence over the way of living and therefore on material culture. These floors, in the raised areas of buildings, nearly always consisted of mats called *tatami*, and their makers were as indispensable as carpenters or plasterers. Illustration 5 shows one of them at work, adding the patterned binding tape round the edges. The *tatami* was approximately 2 m by 1 m and in theory large enough for one person to sleep on. The text above the illustration gives the slightly varying sizes for the Imperial court, the 'three princes' (*sankō*) of the Council of State, and the 'ordinary people's houses' (*minka*) of Western and Eastern Japan. It is noticeable that this order of precedence reflects less strongly in length than in thickness. The Imperial *tatami* were nearly half as thick again as those of the ordinary folk of Eastern Japan (namely the Edo area), though only about 30 cm longer.

The significance of this, of course, is in relative luxury, but all *tatami* performed their function of providing a soft yet firm flooring on which people could sleep, eat, read and write, and do any other indoor activity not involving dirt or mess. For it was and is an absolute rule that no outside footwear should ever be worn on them. Their construction of closely woven reed, filled with rice husks, in a light outer frame provided the firm flexibility needed for comfort, but did not at all allow for easy cleaning.

5. Maker of *tatami* mats, from the stencilled book *Saiga Shokunin Burui* by Minkō, 1770. 285 × 380 mm.

The effects of this type of flooring on interior decoration, the way of

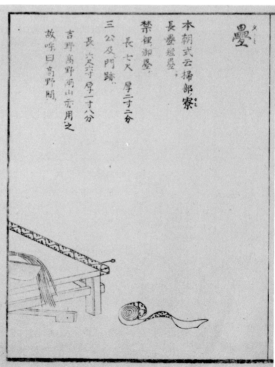
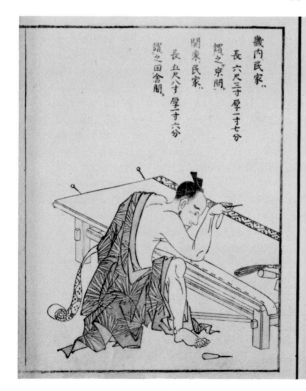

living, and hence of artefacts in general were very great. Firstly, as rooms were measured by the number of *tatami* that formed their floors, there was always a starting-point from which the design of the room had to begin. Not only were their proportions and the various ways in which they locked together known, but also their colour – varying from a fresh, pale green for new ones and fading to a more familiar pale straw colour with age. Since people sat or lay on the floor, objects tended to be small, and their makers, without consciously being aware of it, designed them to harmonise with the background against which they would be seen. We need not look far beyond the *tatami* to explain the relative sobriety of most Japanese boxes, utensils and furniture, and the preference for natural materials, such as wood and bamboo.

The space created by using *tatami* would naturally have been wasted if large furniture had stood on them. That is why the term 'furniture' in Japanese (*chōdo*), when applied to the past, hardly embraces at all the objects Westerners would include under that word. Rather it applies to boxed sets of eating utensils, cosmetics, games, writing or sewing equipment; very low tables; candlesticks and holders; mirror-stands; and portable sets of shelves with little drawers and trays.

A system which was thus designed to make the most of the limited space available to a crowded population obviously could accommodate neither furniture nor the sculptures, busts, or free-standing ornamental ceramic or stone urns, jars and potiches which could be found in a European middle- or upper-class house in the equivalent period.

Larger objects for actual use in Japan were made to be dismantled and stored. The standing screen (*tsuitate*), which at first sight resembles a bulky or even clumsy item of furniture, came apart in this way, and so did the tall lacquered clothes-horses for hanging kimono. Folding screens, which opened out into a length of some 2 m, also came into this category.

All these objects had to be light, because the floor structure would not take too much weight; and they had to be soft in texture, without sharp edges, because the *tatami*, although hard-wearing, could easily be damaged by anything harsh or jagged. The preference for organic materials – wood, bamboo, lacquer, paper, textiles – and their universal predominance in traditional Japanese culture becomes even more understandable in these circumstances of life.

To conform with the *tatami* flooring, with the modular nature of the rooms, and with the taste for organic materials the walls of rooms were made to consist mainly of sliding sections called *shōji*. They were second only to the *tatami* themselves in their influence on the way life was lived indoors. *Shōji* were made from a light lattice wooden framework, a few centimetres thick, over which specially made strong, translucent paper was pasted. It was normally white, pale grey or very pale buff. These sliding doors, as they in fact are, were very similar in height to the length of a *tatami* but they could vary a good deal in width, forming sets of two, four or even more which would constitute a whole inner wall. They could also form an outer wall in fine weather, but outside wooden sliding sections could be fitted in bad conditions. They could even be removed altogether, to make two rooms into one, or to open the house to the outside air in the summer.

6. Maker of brushes, with his trade mark painted on a *tsuitate* screen, from the stencilled book *Saiga Shokunin Burui* by Minkō, 1770. 285 × 190 mm.

Rooms were on the whole quite small, and as glass windows were not used, the *shōji* had to pick up what light there was. In moderate conditions they acted as windows themselves, either full-length, or half-length set in apertures resembling a window in a European house. They could clearly not be decorated in heavy colours without losing their light-giving properties. In the very largest rooms of castles and palaces *shōji* were, from the late sixteenth century onwards, covered in gold leaf and painted, so that the gold could pick up the small amount of light which would filter through into such wide enclosed areas; but in more normal-sized rooms this was not done, and if *shōji* were painted it tended to be in ink only, or very pale colours, leaving plenty of pale background.

On such paper walls there could be no ornaments in the Western sense of the word; that is why the concept of the purely decorative object is virtually unknown in traditional Japan. Only the wooden pillars offered some scope for a little decoration. On them might occasionally be hung a pillar-clock, a lantern, a wall vase for a flower arrangement, a long, thin poem-slip called a *tanzaku*; or, from the mid-eighteenth century onwards in the bourgeois houses of Edo, a similarly shaped pillar-print of topical interest. None of these, however, except perhaps a clock or a lantern, would stay there for more than a day. A pillar was not wide enough for a hanging painting, though some very narrow ones are found which may have been made for that purpose. Hanging paintings had their place in the *tokonoma*, described in Chapter 2.

Above the *shōji* was a beam, and above that was a further area of wall, not usually more than 1 m high, which again might be filled with smaller paper-covered panels, or with wooden panels carved in open-work to let in the light. These were known as *ramma* (see p. 73). The ceiling itself was generally of plain wooden panels, again easily removable, but sometimes in the rooms of the very powerful or the very rich it might be adorned with paper-covered panels decorated with paintings. The pictures of personal possessions, of which one is shown on the cover of this book, show evidence of having been cut out either from ceiling panels of this sort or from small sliding doors from built-in cupboard and shelf fittings. It was not usual to hang lamps from the ceiling, and lighting consisted mostly of lanterns or tall candle-holders which stood on the floor.

Such, then, was the physical context which applied, with some variation, to all urban buildings in Japan except for Shintō shrines and Buddhist temples (see Chapter 3). Since no single object was on permanent view, since lightness and indeed disposability or renewability were prized, and since natural, organic materials were particularly admired, it is not surprising that craftsmanship came to be held in equally high esteem whatever the products and however ephemeral the material. Japan was a land of natural craftsmen, and it needed only money and extensive patronage to stimulate the production of high-quality goods.

The conditions of achieving that stimulation came to exist in a most vigorous way during the sixteenth century and were intensified by the political and social system imposed at the beginning of the seventeenth. Briefly, what happened was a shift from power, influence and social standing to money as the basis of artistic patronage. The growth of this wealth was directly related to the huge and constant expansion of urban

7. A courtesan and her maid relaxing, showing a crowded domestic interior (see p. 85), from the woodblock album *Yoshiwara Keisei Shin Bijin Awase Jihitsu Kagami* by Masanobu, 1784. 382 × 255 mm.

life. The rigid political system imposed by the Tokugawa regime gave the stability, after centuries of internal wars, for the economy to flourish and at the same time accidentally provided an electric social tension which stimulated all the official classes to vie with each other.

Since the introduction of Buddhism and Chinese and Korean culture in the sixth century AD, Japan had been dominated for 1,000 years by various types of power-establishment. In the earliest centuries of that millennium power had been fought over between the Imperial family, the great noble families and the Buddhist priesthood. From the late ninth until the mid-twelfth century power lay with the noble Fujiwara family, who ran a centralised pseudo-Chinese bureaucracy. They were replaced by the rule of the Shogun – the Generalissimo appointed by the Emperor, who dominated by force of arms and was the most powerful of the samurai class. But no shogun was able to hold the country down for long, and the whole period from around 1150 to 1600 can be regarded as a prolonged struggle to achieve military dominance and unite Japan under one government. That was finally achieved by Tokugawa Ieyasu, who defeated his last rivals at the Battle of Sekigahara in 1600 and was appointed Shogun in 1603. His family held office more or less peacefully until 1868.

By then the country had been in political chaos for a century and a half, and some of the great Buddhist establishments had gained virtual independence, with standing armies of their own, and had reasserted themselves as major centres of the arts. However, their suppression began with Oda Nobunaga (1534–1582) and was completed by Ieyasu. Thus Buddhism ceased to be a major patron of the arts and crafts, and many of the artisans who had worked for the temples gradually began to diversify into secular fields. The effect on sculpture was crucial (see Chapter 3).

Nobunaga began the final unification of the country and encouraged the recently arrived European Christian missionaries out of his hatred for Buddhism. Under his rule and that of his successor Toyotomi Hideyoshi (1536–1598) foreign trade with China, South-East Asia, Korea, India and Europe flourished. At that time Japanese traders and pirates roamed the seas of East Asia, and Hideyoshi himself twice invaded Korea. Though they were soon to withdraw into the Isolation, the Japanese had by then absorbed much from the outside world which was to influence their lives and culture. Among those introductions were castles themselves, firearms, clocks, velvets, tobacco and pipes, and card-games from Europe; chintzes, batiks, leatherwork and other new materials from India and South-East Asia; and porcelain, new types of pottery, and printing from movable type from Korea. From China the stream of influence was more constant in all the arts and was to continue throughout the succeeding centuries, with special effects in the decorative arts on miniature sculpture, bronzes and ceramics.

Urban life, that great mixer and vitaliser, was already flourishing in the sixteenth century. The Portuguese missionaries write of the wonders of 'Miyako' (Kyoto), then the centre of both the Emperor and of the Shogun, and headquarters of many of the strongest Buddhist sects, where the streets were perpetually crowded with people and an astonishing array of goods was on sale, and where festivals and entertainments already throve for residents, foreign visitors and pilgrims from within Japan. Kyoto was by

8. *Shō* (mouth-organ). Lacquered bamboo with metal fittings. Late 18th century. L. 40.7 cm.

then by far the greatest city, but others were enjoying a rapid expansion, especially the international ports of Nagasaki and Sakai.

It was, however, the political system of Tokugawa Ieyasu and his two immediate successors that was to make towns and cities the dominant factor in Japanese culture, and it was in them that much of what we now consider 'typically Japanese' grew up. The Tokugawas made three moves producing this result.

The first was Ieyasu's decision to set up his capital in 1590 some 500 km from Kyoto in the great eastern plain known as the Kantō, round a small castle called Edo which had been his for ten years. Edo, a small settlement in the marshes at the mouth of the Sumida River, rapidly grew into a great city which gave its name to the Edo period (1600–1868). It spread out around the huge new castle Ieyasu built there, housing and symbolising the Tokugawa military government. In 1868, at the end of the shoguns' rule, the Emperor finally moved to Edo and it was renamed Tokyo ('the eastern capital').

Secondly, he began the system of *sankin kōtai*, made even stricter after his death, which aimed to control the great *daimyō* or feudal lords. Briefly, it forced all the *daimyō* to maintain great residences called *yashiki* in Edo, where many of them were obliged to spend alternate years with their families, and with large retinues of samurai, sometimes amounting to over 1,000. Those most suspected by the government had to leave their families there all the time. In addition, the shogun's personal retainers, the *hatamoto*, lived in Edo permanently. All had to live up to ceremonial standards, being obliged to attend the shogun on many important occasions. At any one time there were as many as 500,000 such people, including their retainers and servants, and naturally an enormous number of suppliers, merchants, builders, craftsmen and entertainers. Edo grew within a century to become the world's biggest city, constantly attracting new people who were drawn by its life and culture or simply seeking employment or (illegally) fleeing from their agricultural villages.

Thirdly, he placed the *daimyō* in castles throughout Japan, in and around which their samurai retainers had to live. His most favoured lords were put in the largest castles in the most strategic spots – such as Mito, Nagoya and Wakayama. These castle towns all grew during the Edo period and like Edo held a very high proportion of the educated warrior class. They all, therefore, became centres of higher bourgeois rather than lower-class culture. That is one reason why the urban material culture of Japan was of such noticeably high quality compared with ordinary city life elsewhere in the world at that time. The concentration of the samurai in urban centres led to a similar concentration of craftsmen there.

To serve the complex internal commodity and money systems which became essential because of this way of life the city of Osaka grew very fast, acting as a depot for the whole country. It soon overtook Kyoto in population, and by the late seventeenth century Japan was dominated by the three great cities of Edo, Osaka and Kyoto, each with its own pride, its own styles and its own cultural specialities.

It is clear that this state of affairs was likely to lead to a great increase in local production and an improvement in internal trade, and that is probably what the far-sighted Ieyasu intended. To equip the large population of samurai – and they amounted in the seventeenth century to about one-tenth of the population of around twenty-five million – with even the ceremonial armour, swords, fittings, bows and horse-trappings necessary for their journeys to Edo required master-craftsmen in large numbers. To build their mansions, to dress their ladies and to provide the rich textiles and lacquers needed to maintain their status in life required many more. To pay for these extravagances the *daimyō* were forced to encourage their local products. As a result of this came the great development, for example, of the porcelain industry in the fiefs of the Matsuura and Nabeshima *daimyō* in the island of Kyūshū, and the spread of textile production, pottery, paper-making and mining into many new areas of the country. All this in turn led to the rise on an unprecedented scale in the wealth and numbers of townsmen of the non-samurai class, for the samurai were not allowed to take part in trade (at least not officially) and they and the Tokugawas themselves needed bankers, middle-men, engineers, transport experts and managers of every sort.

Here an explanation should be given of the official social system imposed by the Tokugawas, known in Japanese as *Shinōkōshō*, from the four written characters for samurai, farmer, craftsman and tradesman. This was the order of precedence, and it put the 'tradesmen', which included the very richest and most powerful merchants, at the bottom of the pile. Naturally they tried to emulate their social betters, but repressive laws against display kept their taste on the whole quieter than it might have been given a free rein. Indeed, many of them were led to support the Tea Ceremony, Confucian learning, the *Nō* theatre and other respectable pursuits such as painting and calligraphy, the incense-game, classical music and poetry.

Rich farmers, thriving on sought-after cash crops such as tobacco, silk, lacquer, cotton and sugar, gradually joined in this way of life, as did the great craftsmen who grew more and more prosperous supplying the needs for refined and expensive goods. So, too, did those who did not even fall into the class system at all – the actors, puppeteers, popular musicians and singers, entertainers, wrestlers and prostitutes who throve in the great cities. Most of them were major patrons of the crafts – especially textiles, miniature carving, lacquering and colour-printing – and even of swords and elaborate fittings, for those who were rich and respectable enough were permitted to wear one sword, in contrast to the samurai's two.

In this restless urban world variety and novelty came to be increasingly important, so it was inevitable that local products should be sought after. The increase in wealth allowed people to travel, and the *daimyō* and merchants took every chance to sell and popularise their local wares. The thirst for knowledge of the scenery and products of Japan can be measured by the ever-growing numbers of books and prints published about them. It is significant that until the mid-eighteenth century books and prints about the three great cities predominated, and they were obviously taken home as souvenirs of the glittering and exciting urban life which country visitors encountered. After that, however, there is a great increase in the numbers of publications about the rest of Japan, more obviously slanted towards city dwellers whose own horizons were widening. The books, *meishoki* ('records of famous places'), often go into great detail about local products.

The now celebrated woodblock sheet-prints of Hokusai (1760–1849),

Hiroshige (1797–1858) and their followers were born of this desire by the citizens of Edo to have views of the famous places of Japan, and incidentally of their products. Hiroshige's well-known series of views along the great roads of the Tōkaidō and the Kisokaidō, both taking different routes from Edo to Kyoto, show the teeming life at the posting-stations on the way, where almost every one had a local product to sell. Those products were often gastronomic, but they also included more lasting mementoes. Yabuhara, on the Kisokaidō, for example, made fine hair-combs of *minebari* (a birch-wood).

The great comic writer Jippensha Ikku (1766–1831) also records the endless selling along the Tōkaidō road in his novel *Hizakurige* (1802). At Ōmori, not far from Edo, he tells of the straw-plaiting carried on in every house; in Kyoto, the source of everything most refined, of textiles, make-up and fans, and of the perversely artistic inhabitants who would eat the poorest food out of magnificent lacquered vessels; and in Osaka of the countless articles on sale, brought by ships from all parts of Japan. At Yamada in Ise he tells of the pilgrims who came in their thousands to the Great Shrines. Such pilgrims must have bought the netsuke made by Masanao and his school in that town. A similar story is told a century earlier in the novels of Ihara Saikaku (1642–93), and a century before that in the accounts of European visitors – a continuous story of brisk production, constant travelling and trade, and intense feeling for quality and novelty.

Japan could then as now be called a land of craftsmen, and the interest in technique was intense, especially among the well-off merchant class. A vivid example of that interest was the book *Saiga Shokunin Burui* ('Various classes of artisans in coloured pictures') by Tachibana Minkō published in two volumes in Edo in 1770, and itself the result of the crafts of woodblock cutting (for the outline) and stencilling (for the colour). It shows craftsmen at work, each accompanied by a short descriptive text about the techniques involved. Where possible it mentions the historical origins of a particular craft, for in Japan skill was associated with the Shintō religion, and every craft or profession had its particular *kami* or god, who represented the spirit of the technique or of the material itself. Some craftsmen, like woodworkers and swordsmiths, claimed particularly ancient lineage, and as can be seen (10) they wore Shintō ceremonial robes and hats for the crucial parts of their work. This special relationship with materials is very Japanese, and modern craftsmen who carry on the old traditions speak of 'understanding the spirit' of a working substance through long acquaintance and respect. In the pre-modern period such thoughts were not written down but they cannot have been very different. Confirmation comes, in the related field of painting, from the Osaka artist Mori Sosen (1747–1821) who we know to have spent several years alone in the mountains studying the apes of which he became the greatest depictor.

This is not to imply, however, that most Japanese craftsmen were lone seekers after perfection as some of their modern counterparts are. Rather they were organised into family/workshop groups, with a master-craftsman who gave his name to the final product but by no means did all the work, and who would in any case be involved only in the most skilled or artistic parts of a process. Thus a master lacquerer such as Koma Kansai II

9. Twisting braids from *Saiga Shokunin Burui* by Minkō, 1770. 285 × 190 mm.

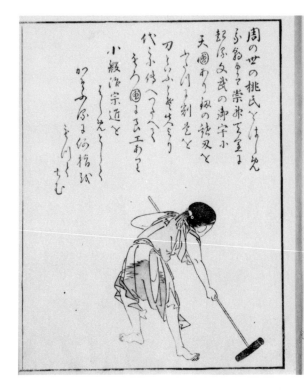

治鍛

10. Swordsmith from the stencilled book *Saiga Shokunin Burui* by Minkō, 1770. 285 × 380 mm.

(1766–1835) would not be involved in the preparing of the shaped wooden or paper base of, for example, a seal-case nor in the various applications of lacquer as a ground; nor even in the decorative sprinkling of gold-leaf flakes to produce the effect of a starry sky often used for the insides of compartments. Rather his contribution would be the elaborate decoration in gold and other coloured lacquers applied at the end. Nevertheless, the piece would go out under his signature. He might even supply only the basic idea of the design, which would then be executed by his most experienced pupils. He and they would naturally have learned all the other processes earlier in their careers; and poor work by the apprentices at any level would be immediately detected by the more experienced craftsmen. A common pride in the name of the workshop was thus held by all. This was reinforced by the habit of bestowing the family name itself by a form of adoption on those pupils, not already related by blood to the head of the family, who had reached the high standards required.

An even more elaborate system operated in arts, crafts and professions of national prestige, such as the Kanō painters, the Gotō metalworkers and the Kōami lacquerers. All of these were officially appointed by the shogunate, but were able to license sub-schools elsewhere in Japan to use their name. The head of the whole 'family' was known as the *iemoto* ('origin of the house'), and this *iemoto* system was particularly important in the Edo period, both in spreading standards of craftsmanship and, in the end, in standardising and monopolising practice to such an extent that inspiration died. The many individualists who broke away from their masters in the first half of the nineteenth century were a natural result.

A list of the products illustrated in *Saiga Shokunin Burui* (1770) is most illuminating about the applied arts of the time. They are (in the order given) ceremonial hats; mirrors; woodwork; swords; sewing armour; silk braids; twisted-paper braids for dressing the hair; woven gold brocades; paper-making; sword-fittings; bamboo blinds (*sudare*); leather quivers; plaited bamboo baskets; leather footballs; blown glass; folding fans; the *koto*; masks; writing brushes; Raku pottery; *tatami* mats; lathe-turned wooden objects; mounting of hanging paintings; playing-cards; paper umbrellas; stone handmills; needles; and inkstones. The most prestigious crafts come at the beginning, and the first four had special status.

Although this selection is an individual one and leaves many crafts out, it is a fair representation of what was admired in 1770 in the mid-Edo period. It is significant that of the twenty-eight listed nineteen are concerned with organic materials, one (sewing armour) partly with organic materials and partly with metal, and only eight with inorganic (stone, metal, ceramics and glass).

It is also very noticeable that of the four commonest types of Japanese object found in Western collections – porcelain, sword-fittings, lacquer *inrō* and carved netsuke – only one (sword-fittings) is thought worthy of inclusion. That is because of the high esteem in which everything to do with the samurai's sword was held. The absences are partly a reflection of the difference between native and foreign emphasis, for several of the craftsmen are actually depicted wearing *inrō* and netsuke as if they were quite taken for granted. They were, however, shortly to be written about extensively for the first time in an Osaka book of 1781 (see Chapter 3). Porcelain had not yet become widespread over Japan as it was to do in the following generation (see Chapter 5).

Porcelain, glass and playing-cards are all products resulting from influence from outside Japan. The period 1600–1900 encloses in it the Isolation which for practical purposes lasted from 1639 until 1853, when foreign contacts were at a minimum. Before 1639 and after 1853, however, there were periods of very intense foreign influence and infiltration. The arts of these three centuries, then, have to be seen in the context of a very strong contrast and struggle between native and foreign attitudes. This is discussed in more detail in Chapter 5, for it is in ceramics that this interplay was strongest.

Although this book is concerned with Japanese decorative arts, it does not try to define Japanese decorative style, for that is likely to lead to confusing generalisations which cannot apply uniformly to the products of a populous, energetic, inventive nation over a period of three eventful centuries. Nevertheless, some discussions of stylistic trends are given in the chapters on lacquer and porcelain; and a close look at the illustrations should emphasise certain very broad tendencies in Japanese craftsmanship which could be described as national. Among them are a very deep feeling for the natural world and the seasons; respect for the quality of materials; close observation of people, wild creatures, plants and man-made objects without the analytical approach found in the West; and in design itself a fondness for the use of blank space, combined with an at times breathtaking ability to place a subject on the surface in the most perfect and yet unstrained manner.

2 METALWORK

Decorative Japanese metalwork developed along three distinct lines: first, castable metals, chiefly bronze, which were used to make images and temple and household vessels; iron and steel which supplied the forges of tool- and weapon-makers; finally, the fine decorative work which reached a peak of ornamentation in the nineteenth century and had developed from the work in precious metals that adorned the swords of the samurai.

Bronze and similar alloys

By the seventh century AD the Japanese had learned from the continent of East Asia how to make fine-quality bronze castings of Buddhist images and other paraphernalia by the lost-wax method, and this remained the major use of bronze until the Edo period. The lost-wax method, which originated in the Middle East *c.* 3000 BC, arrived in the Far East with Buddhist bronze images in the early centuries AD and was used in Japan from the introduction of Buddhism in the late sixth century AD. It involved building a core of framework and clay on which the interior surface of the object was modelled. The whole was covered with wax, in which the external surface of the object was modelled. After coating again with sufficient clay to form an outer mould which was then dried, the whole was heated so that the wax melted away leaving a hollow space into which the molten metal was poured. After cooling, the mould was removed and the piece finished by hand. For repetitive products, such as vessels or popular images, the mould was made in two halves so that it could be removed without breaking and reused. This method often left a ridge of metal along the join of the two halves; for the best pieces this might be filed away and polished. In cheaper objects the ridge was left, but sometimes it was incorporated into a design which masked it.

The constituents of Japanese bronzes varied considerably: whereas bronzes for images were often more than 90 per cent copper with most of the remainder tin, a characteristic of the alloys used for vases and other ornamental wares was the inclusion of lead in amounts from a few per cent up to 20. Compared with the straightforward copper–tin mixture, these alloys possess greater fluidity in melt, lower melting-point and less contraction upon solidification, and therefore reproduce intricate detail more faithfully. The presence of lead also gives a soft lustre to the surface. The most important colouring agent, however, was the alloy known as *shirome*, a mixture of arsenic and antimony in alloy with varying amounts of silver, copper and lead, which could be obtained as a by-product of the separation of silver from copper by liquation with lead. *Shirome* added to a whole range of bronzes and other alloys containing copper allowed the creation of beautiful dark patinas produced by various pickling processes. These employed many varied ingredients, usually kept secret and passed on by oral tradition, and the methods are not yet fully understood; common to all, however, was the length of time needed to achieve the effects and the very exact control of the ingredients based on experience. Intermediate polishing or washing also played an important part.

Imported Chinese bronzes bearing the Xuande reign mark (1426–35) gave a name to the brass-like alloy containing copper, tin and zinc called in Japanese *sentoku*, which is written with the same Chinese characters as Xuande. This alloy was often used for Chinese-style cast objects. *Shinchū*, or *odō*, was another brass containing copper and zinc. It was used on Buddhist objects because of its resemblance to gold and on mechanisms such as guns and clocks because it could be engineered with precision and did not corrode easily.

The monasteries were by far the most important patrons of the products of bronze casting but they had lost much of their wealth and power during the civil wars of the fifteenth and sixteenth centuries, and apart from the manufacture of a limited number of bells and images, often to replace items damaged in fire and earthquake, there was little large-scale religious bronzework of artistic significance made during the days of the Tokugawas. There were, however, enough impressive cast lamps, *shishi* (guardian lion dogs) and architectural decorations produced for official projects like the magnificent shrine to Ieyasu at Nikkō to prove that the basic skills had not been lost. The newly rich townsmen began to commission small images both for use on household altars and for donation to temples in order to secure spiritual benefit for themselves and their families (see Chapter 3). In spite of the decline of Buddhist metal sculpture, and particularly large-scale sculpture in the Edo period, bronze and brass items were made in ever larger quantities. The most important of these were vases, incense-burners, mirrors and Buddhist paraphernalia.

The proliferation of the Tea Ceremony, which accompanied increased prosperity, was probably responsible in some measure for the greater use of the *tokonoma* alcove in ordinary houses, where a vase of ceramic, woven bamboo or bronze would be used for a flower arrangement. Bronze vases of many different forms were made throughout the Edo period, many in imitation of Chinese bronzes or ceramics and usually stamped with Chinese-style seal characters. Some were made in more typically Japanese shapes, resembling in their apparent roughness the pottery vases for the Tea Ceremony or even imitating woven bamboo. In the second half of the nineteenth century vases were made which were very much more accomplished in techniques and with a wide variety of shapes. They often had elaborate patinated surfaces, or were engraved with pictorial designs, or inlaid with silver, gold or other alloys. At their best these pieces are elegant, but from the fact that so many are in Western houses it is clear that they were made primarily for export as flower-vases or ornaments in European taste (29).

The Tea Ceremony also encouraged the use of incense, hitherto confined to Buddhist temples and the very rich. Bronze was one of the main materials for making incense-burners. The burner consisted of a vessel of almost any shape, usually on legs (to protect the surface on which it stood from the heat) and with a perforated lid to let the smoke escape. In the Edo period burners became more elaborate, and those in bronze or iron were often made in the shape of an animal or bird, with holes in the eyes or between the wings used to emit the smoke. Part of the top, of course, had to be detachable so that the incense could be inserted, and this and the above-mentioned holes are clues that a bronze vessel is indeed a burner (11).

The mirror was an object of high prestige because together with the sword and sacred jewel it made up the Imperial regalia. Makers of mirrors therefore held particularly high status in the artisan class and, like swordsmiths, were sometimes awarded honorary noble titles which they used with their signatures. An example is the title *kami*, which is an ancient court appointment at local level. 'Kami of Satsuma' therefore means not literally a local lord but a craftsman given the theoretical status of that appointment because of the quality of his craft.

Until the Muromachi period mirrors were predominantly round, sometimes with a foliate rim, and those for domestic use were typically about 9 cm in diameter. These cast-bronze mirrors had a boss in the centre with a hole through which a carrying cord passed, but this fell out of use following the introduction of handles, which were until the early Edo period brazed on to the edge of the mirror.

The central boss was traditionally in the form of a tortoise, a symbol of long life and happiness, and the design on the back of the mirror was symmetrical about this boss. After dispensing with the boss during the seventeenth century, the artist was free to spread his composition all over the mirror. The favoured designs included landscapes, traditional motifs derived from Chinese symbolism such as the auspicious group of cranes in pines, *mon* (family crests), geometric patterns and human figures. During the late seventeenth century mirrors illustrated with people at work became popular among the richer townsfolk, and the size became larger in order to accommodate the built-up hair-styles of the ladies. Handles became shorter, and those of old mirrors were frequently cut down to suit the new fashion.

12. Bronze hand-mirror with a man punting a log by water. Inscribed Tenkaichi. Late 17th century. DIAM. 21.4 cm.

Mirror-makers were one of the craftsmen guilds from which it had been the custom since the late sixteenth century to elect one man as 'Tenka-Ichi', or 'The First under the Heavens'. This inscription is found on mirrors of the Momoyama and early Edo periods, but its use was prohibited by the government in 1682 owing to excessive use by unauthorised makers. This, however, seems to have had little effect, and many mirrors of nineteenth-century date bear the inscription, which had by then become meaningless as a guarantee of quality.

Shortly following the prohibition of the title 'Tenka-Ichi' it became widespread practice for mirror-makers to present mirrors to the Imperial palaces and receive titulary honours in return. Such widespread use of noble titles by artisans again offended the Tokugawas, who prohibited their use. However, the mirror-founders petitioned the court, and an Imperial decree of 1772 overruled the shogun's order; but as in the case of the 'Tenka-Ichi', such titles came to have no meaning as a guide to quality. As in all Japanese arts and crafts, a title or signature without quality is worth little.

The better-quality mirrors of the seventeenth century were made in moulds modelled in fine clays mixed with *tonoko* (polishing dust) and baked hard. The cast mirrors had to be polished smooth on the reflecting face, and this was the longest part of the manufacturing process. High-tin bronzes could be polished to form a white surface, but the more common alloys consisting almost wholly of copper had to be tinned using mercury amalgam.

In the eighteenth and nineteenth centuries mirrors became increasingly used by poorer people, and both quality of product and design declined in the mass-production foundries. These mass-produced mirrors were made using the methods of the mint, by pressing patterns into sand to make the moulds. Sometimes old mirrors were used in this repetitive greensand moulding process, with the signatures erased or changed.

The mirror became widely used as a wedding gift, the designs becoming indicative of longevity, happiness, procreation, and so on. Large written characters in a flowing calligraphic style were introduced to supplement the pictorial matter, so that one might find, for example, an illustration of bamboo together with the written character for 'tiger', referring to the common Buddhist motif of a tiger or tigers in a bamboo grove.

Among other bronze items made in some numbers in the Edo period are Buddhist ritual objects. They include small hand-bells and *vajra* (ceremonial thunderbolts) as held by the terrifying deities of tantric (or magical) Buddhism which are sometimes gilt. Pierced and engraved gilt-bronze fittings for boxes to hold the scriptures continued to be made and usually represent lotus flowers or leaves. Similar fittings are found on the cylindrical sutra-holders carried by wandering priests. All of these items were thoroughly traditional in design, and because of that are often dated far earlier than they should be by optimistic collectors. They are fairly commonly found in the West because so many left Japan in the late nineteenth century when Buddhism was in deep decline there.

Iron and steel

The production of iron was by a simple and time-consuming low-temperature smelting process. The ore, known as *satetsu* (sand iron) was sandwiched in layers alternating with charcoal over a hole in the ground and the furnace built around it. The draught was supplied through holes at the sides using a tread-bellows which required six or eight men working continuously for three or four days and nights, during which time a critical eye had to be kept on the temperature. The resulting sponge of iron was of high purity and low in carbon, and could easily be broken up for distribution and further treatment.

Iron was mostly mechanically worked, and steel was produced from it by the swordsmith, gunsmith, or blacksmith at his forge. Initially the main iron refiners in the seventeenth century were the warrior clans such as the Tabe, Sakurai and Itōhara of the Chūgoku area and the Sasaki of Hiroshima, because the main use of iron was for arms. Throughout the Edo period, however, the development of the economy depended not a little on the distribution of iron agricultural instruments, and towards the end of the seventeenth century a district of iron-founders, the Tetsuza, was established in Ōsaka with commercial capital. Various technical innovations at the Tetsuza included the adoption of an efficient lever-bellows, which required only two operators, and permanent furnaces housed in foundry buildings. Guns, bladed weapons and farm tools alike were made by forging iron and steel.

In the middle of the nineteenth century some of the more warlike *daimyō*, alarmed at the might of Western navies, built, using Western technology, the first high-temperature blast-furnaces to make the large amounts of iron needed for big guns. One *daimyō*, Nariaki of Satsuma, had a furnace built within his castle grounds and used it for making glass and ceramics, in addition to iron. A further form of iron, *nambantetsu*, was imported in the early period in small amounts from several different places in Asia. The term *namban* means 'southern barbarian' and was used of almost anything imported via South-East Asia or South China by either Asians or Europeans.

Some casting of low-carbon iron was done for Buddhist images, pans and tea kettles. The form of the squat globular iron kettle for the Tea Ceremony with two carrying handles had become standard during the Muromachi period. No spout was necessary, since in the ceremony water was taken from the large aperture at the top in a ladle and transferred to individual tea bowls. The kettle in fact sat on its charcoal burner throughout, and since water was carried to it to fill it, its weight and size were of no practical disadvantage. Ware from the two main centres of manufacture, Ashiya in Chikuzen (modern Fukuoka Prefecture) and Temmyō in Sano city (modern Ibaraki Prefecture), was marketed all over the country. The increase in popularity of the Tea Ceremony led to the establishment of a kettle-foundry district at Sanjō in Kyoto in the seventeenth century, and it was here that wares made in conformity with the tastes of the tea masters such as Sen-no-Rikyū and Furuta no Oribe were produced and took the market from Temmyō and Ashiya during the Edo period.

The kettles were cast in two halves, top and bottom, using the lost-wax method, with the base section inverted so that the molten iron reached the widest part first. Evidence of this is visible in the mark in the centre of the base of a kettle indicating the position of the mouth of the mould. Tradition dictated that kettles should appear ancient and sombre, and this effect was obtained by softening the casting and treating the surface mechanically to give it a rugged appearance, or by hot corrosion using plum vinegar, iron oxide, lacquer and other materials to produce lasting black or brown patinas.

The same method was used to make the smaller kettles with spouts and overhead handles which are far more recognisable to Western eyes for what they are. They were not used for the Tea Ceremony proper but rather for ordinary infused green tea. They were often inlaid with designs in gold and silver which stood out brilliantly on the black iron, and their lids were invariably of a high-copper bronze. Such kettles are often found in Western collections made in the second half of the nineteenth century or the early twentieth century, but the true Tea Ceremony kettles are rarely found, since they were both difficult to transport and to appreciate.

The most important use for iron and steel during the period was in the production of arms and armour. The several styles of traditional Japanese armour in use until the second half of the sixteenth century consisted of loosely linked iron or leather pieces joined with silk braid in the form of construction known as *odoshi*. Although this construction was light and flexible, allowing ease of movement, and was proof against stray arrows

13. Tea kettle. Cast iron with a vine arbour inlaid in gold and silver, the lid bronze, inscribed Ryūbundō. 19th century. H. excluding handle 12.2 cm.

14. Suit of armour. Iron and lacquered iron plate on textile. The cuirass, signed Unkai Mitsunao, c. 1600; the remainder 18th century. H. as mounted 1.25 m.

and glancing sword cuts, it was little use against firearms. For this reason cuirasses of heavy plate in the European manner were introduced to replace the old styles; some of this armour of the Momoyama period was actually made from suits imported from Europe.

The sleeves and skirt remained unchanged: armpieces consisted of light plates linked with chain-mail and sewn on to textile sleeves, and the skirts remained as hanging sections of plates loosely joined with braid. The looseness of construction is vividly shown by the ease with which a whole suit of armour can be packed into a small box. The helmet was considered the most important part of an armour, and it was here that the best craftsmanship is seen. Helmets were made of a number of plates shaped and riveted together, and it is not unusual to find examples with thirty-two, sixty-four, or more than 100 such plates joined along vertical seams which meet at the hole in the crown. Face masks of forged iron plate were separate and tied on to the face with the helmet cords. Made by the helmet-makers, like helmets they could be either iron patinated to russet brown or lacquered in red or black. Sometimes whiskers were attached to give added ferocity.

Armours of the Momoyama period were often grotesquely decorated expressing the wearer's individuality. Some, both humorous and terrifying, were in the form of beasts and monsters, and helmets were made surmounted with horns or dragon heads, or even sword blades. During the peace of the Edo period, however, armour was used almost solely for procession and ceremony. The outlandish styles of the Momoyama period were frowned upon and rejected by the authorities in favour of more conformist wear. The highest-ranking samurai wore light armour in the ancient ōyoroi style, and their retinues wore simple uniform suits of armour more for show than service. Even so many good armours were made during the Edo period, notably under the revivalist movement in the early nineteenth century (see p. 36). Some makers like the Iwai and Haruta families were employed by the government, but others like the Myōchin family were free enterprisers dispersed over the country.

The Myōchin family name is often found on iron sword guards of the late Edo period, but it is likely that many of the artists who made these had never forged plate armour. Their inroads into the open market included the production of models of animals, birds, fish and dragons formed from artfully joined plates of iron articulating in a lifelike manner (15).

15. Articulated model of a crayfish. Russet iron. Signed Myōchin Muneaki. 19th century. L. with feelers extended 67.5 cm.

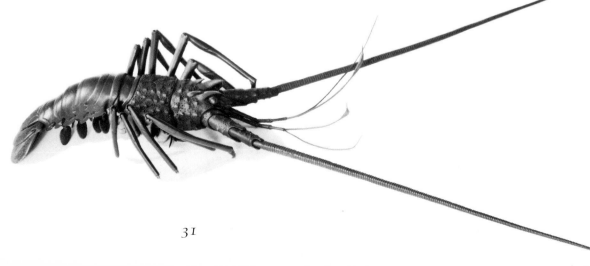

Although the Japanese had experienced explosive devices in warfare when the armies of the Mongols had attempted invasion in the thirteenth century there was no use of firearms until the introduction of matchlock guns by the first Portuguese visitors in 1543. These guns were immediately copied and manufactured in great quantity. Known as 'Tanegashima' guns after the island where they were first seen, they played a considerable part in the wars of unification over the following half-century and in Hideyoshi's Korean campaigns in the 1590s. Indeed, the use of heavy guns gave birth to the Japanese castle, which had been unnecessary until then since only hand-weapons were used.

The basic shape and workings of these guns remained largely unchanged during the Edo period and, apart from limited experimentation, there was

16. Matchlock gun. Wood with a steel barrel decorated with dragons in silver overlay, and the *mon* of the Tokugawas in gold. Signed 'Yoshiyuki lord of Echizen' and dated equivalent to 1685. Overall L. 1.02 m.

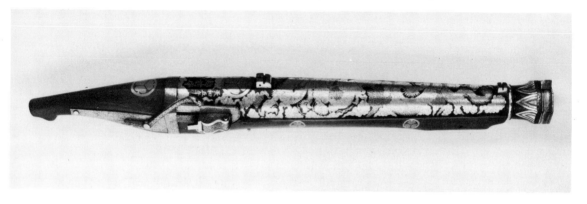

no development beyond the simple matchlock until the second half of the nineteenth century. There was, after all, little need for guns in an era of peace and isolation, and besides the samurai had an aversion to guns which, it was felt, lowered the tone of warfare. For this reason and because of government regulations gun-making had become very limited by the end of the seventeenth century.

Apart from some horse pistols and the *hiyato*, or 'burning arrow gun', of bronze, used mainly in marine warfare, the barrels were made by wrapping iron sheets around a mandrel. The Kunitomo village of Chōshū and Sakai in Izumi became centres for gun-making on a commercial scale during the early seventeenth century, and at first the stronger *daimyō* sponsored their own smiths. The Kunitomo makers used several layers of sheet to produce heavy improved weapons, but the very finest barrels were made by a more complex method whereby iron ribbons were welded in opposed spirals, sometimes in conjunction with steel, to form strong composite structures.

Different craftsmen produced the locks from brass, though iron was sometimes used. In a typical gun of this sort the serpentine was cocked against a spring and released by pulling the trigger so as to apply the match to the touch-hole. The pan had a brass cover which had to be moved aside manually on the standard type, and the pivot on the cover was sometimes provided with a vertical hole into which a leather shield could be inserted to keep the lock dry during rain. The sights fixed to the barrel were provided with small holes into which sticks of glowing incense could be stuck for aiming at night. Smaller than the original European pattern, the wooden stock was not held to the shoulder but against the cheek, although heavier weapons were held tucked into the armpit. The barrels of guns were often inlaid with the same motifs as were engraved on some sword blades – dragons, thunderbolts and the warlike deity Fudō. Silver and gold, occasionally copper, were used for these inlays, which are rather similar technically to those found on the small spouted tea kettles (p. 28).

The principal weapon of the samurai was the sword. It held such a place of symbolic importance that the saying 'the sword is the soul of the samurai' became almost literally interpreted by the Japanese. For more than 1,000 years it has maintained its place as the most perfect cutting weapon to be found in the world. Its technical excellence derives from the method of manufacture involving the continuous folding and welding

17. Pair of stirrups. Iron with peonies in silver inlay, and inlaid inside with mother-of-pearl in lacquer. Signed by Shigetsugu of Osaragi. 18th century. L. 28.8 cm; H. 25.5 cm.

together of billets of high-purity steels, which results in a blade of complex cross-section with a resilient centre and a hard and rigid skin. The edge is further hardened by a heat treatment involving raising the temperature of the whole blade to red heat and quenching it in water. The grain due to the folding process and the crystalline structures formed by the heat treatment become visible when the blade is skilfully polished with stones, and apart from the overall shape it is largely in the appearance of these two effects that the intrinsic beauty of the sword lies.

Forging grain can be either parallel (*masame*), or with the appearance of wood grain (*itame*), or like a wood grain with concentric whirls (*mokume*). Usually the grain is a mixture of these types. The crystalline structure that defines the hardened edge of the sword is called the *hamon*, which forms a continuous line, straight or undulating in a variety of patterns along the curve of the blade, to turn back at the point. According to the size of the

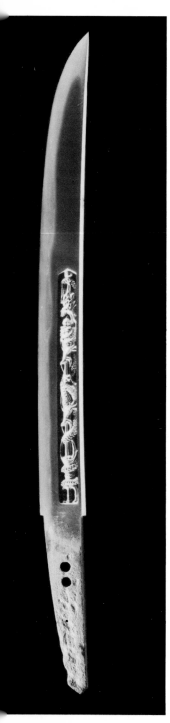

18A. Dagger blade pierced and carved in Kinai style with motif of dragon and *vajra* (thunderbolt)-hilted sword. *Hamon* of 'wild undulating' *nie*. False inscription of Masamune, but an Echizen sword, probably by Yasutsugu I. *c.* 1600. L. excluding tang 30.2 cm.

steel crystals in the *hamon*, it is classified as *nie* (boiling), if the crystals are visible to the naked eye, or *nioi* (fragrance), a cloudy white continuity in which the individual crystals cannot be distinguished with the naked eye. Both *nie* and *nioi* can be present on the flat of the blade, interrelated with the changing direction of the folding grain and the dispersion of different carbon levels in the mixed steels. *Nie* on the flat is called *jinie*, and *nioi* is called *shirake* (or *utsuri* when it occurs as a sort of reflection of the *hamon*).

Whatever their length, the blades were usually single-edged and usually curved, although some daggers were straight. They included the long sword (*tachi* or *katana*), companion sword (*wakizashi*) with a shorter blade, and daggers for ladies, high-ranking samurai and retired gentlemen. Spears (*yari*) and glaives (*naginata*) were made by the same process as swords, but most Edo-period examples are of poor quality and intended primarily for use in processions of *daimyō* and their retainers.

Swords made after the first year of Keichō (1596) are in Japan designated as *shintō* ('new swords' – this term is not the same word as Shintō, meaning the native Japanese religion, and written in different characters), as opposed to *kotō* (old swords) made before that date. The difference was a matter of both technology and style and resulted from the change in society brought about by the victory of the Tokugawa family.

Of the several broad traditions of sword-making which had in some cases been unbroken for hundreds of years, towards the end of the sixteenth century the schools of Bizen and Mino had virtually monopolised the market with vast productions of blades which were serviceable yet inferior in quality to those of the eleventh to fifteenth centuries. The Mino smiths seem to have perfected methods of making sound blades relatively easily, perhaps owing to developments in furnace technology associated with the potter's art or experience in gun-making. Their confidence and pride in workmanship is evidenced by the fact that they each used their own signature, usually with one character, *kane*, derived from the name of Kaneuji, the fourteenth-century master of the school. Moreover, the Mino smiths were the *ujiko* (parishioners) of the Kasuga shrines, a network of prestigious centres of the Shintō religion which had always particularly patronised crafts and professions. This bond must also have been partly responsible for the development of metalworking in the province and the freedom with which the smiths were able to travel and set up forges in the new castle towns at the turn of the sixteenth and seventeenth centuries. Sword-making during the early Edo period developed in every region with new schools under the strong influence of the Mino style.

In the decades of extravagant luxury enjoyed by the military class and the more powerful of the rice merchants during the Momoyama period, high-ranking samurai vied with each other for possession of the most noble luxury of all, a fine old sword. These old cavalry swords were cut down to a size convenient for carrying and were thrust through the belt edge upwards in the style of the day. The mountings of these swords were extravagant, and the more influential of the samurai established styles lasting beyond their day. Hideyoshi himself had worn a pair of swords in vermilion scabbards decorated with broad helical stripes of solid gold.

Specialist craftsmen were employed to cut down the old blades from up to 150 cm to a convenient 70 cm or so. These blades were naturally broad

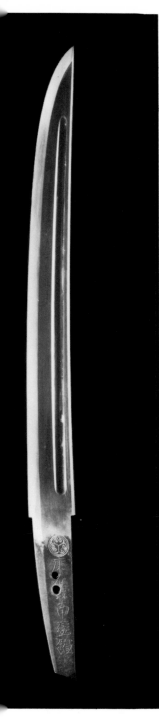

in keeping with their original length and when cut down retained their broad shape with a shallow curve and a bold long point. This was the pattern for the early *shintō* swords made by the first generations of smiths in the new castle towns.

Among the significant smiths of this early period Yasutsugu of Echizen was patronised by Ieyasu in Edo itself. He and his school were employed in making swords, repairing swords damaged by fire and producing copies of old swords for presentation. Many of his copies were of the works of the fourteenth-century school of Masamune of Sōshū, which were rich in *nie*. Masamune was the most admired of all swordsmiths, and the imitations of his work, as well as straightforward fakes, are very numerous at all periods. Indeed, the Sōshū-style *hamon* was universally popular in the Edo period, and it may be said that *shintō* swords are characterised by the bold beauty of *nie*. Also in Edo Nōda Hankei, who had originally been a gunsmith, made swords whose steel resembled that of Norishige, the pupil of Masamune.

In Kyoto, home of the Yamashiro tradition of centuries before, Umetada Myōjū made daggers in imitation of the finest old work with undulating *hamon* of fine *nie*. Myōjū was a versatile metalworker and respected appraiser of old blades, and young smiths flocked to his forge to learn his secrets. Among his pupils were the *Sampin* brothers (Kanemichi, Yoshimichi and Masatoshi) and Horigawa Kunihiro and his close students Kuniyasu and Kunimichi, whose work was so good that it was easily mistaken for that of the school of Masamune and others. One notable smith who was apprentice to Myōjū for just three years was Tadayoshi, retained by the lord of Nabeshima. Successive generations of his school produced fine-quality swords with the same bright fine-grain steel known as *konuka hada* (the rice powder used as a facial cosmetic) and typically a straight *hamon*, though undulating and clove flower patterns are found on some of their work.

In Sendai, in Northern Japan, Kunikane forged swords with *masame* grain in the style of the ancient Hōshō school of Yamato. In Osaka the smiths Kunisada, Kunisuke and their pupils thrived during the first decades, and other smiths became established in Wakamatsu, Hiroshima, Kanazawa, Nagoya and the other castle towns. The old Bizen tradition persisted in the Ishidō school, with branches in Edo, Osaka and elsewhere.

After a few decades the style of swords changed considerably. Most samurai were in the service of the *daimyō* and the government, but the civil wars ending in 1615 had left a dangerous minority of samurai without masters. These *rōnin* (wave men) were a source of possible insurrection against the Tokugawas, and certainly of local disorder. Thousands had, for example, joined Hideyori, the son of Hideyoshi, in his stand against Ieyasu at the seige of Osaka castle in 1615. A series of edicts was published aiming at restricting the behaviour of the *rōnin* and emphasising the position of the retained samurai in society. Regulations prohibited the wearing of very long swords, outlandish costume and hair-styles, and eventually it became in 1651 illegal for a retained samurai to employ any *rōnin*. Samurai in service were required to wear their hair in the standard *chonmage* style with a carefully dressed topknot, to wear the uniform *kamishimo* dress, which consisted of a divided skirt and jacket over

18B. Dagger blade with a single groove. *Hamon* of 'undulating' *nie*. Inscribed with the Tokugawa *mon*. Signed 'By Yasutsugu [II] in Edo using imported steel'. Early 17th century. L. excluding tang 36.9 cm.

a white undergarment, and to carry a pair of swords of restricted length with lacquered black scabbards when on duty in the capital.

This was the background to the style of blade made from around the middle of the seventeenth century. The curve became shallower and the blade decreased in width towards the point. The shape also owed much to the forms of sword-play which thrived in the castle towns. The deep curve and heavy blade had little place in 'academy' fencing, which had come to replace real warfare.

Edo had a very high population of samurai, their numbers made up of the Tokugawas' own garrison and swelled by the retinues of the *daimyō* obliged to visit for six months in the year. Against this formal and military background the major swordsmiths of the period, Kotetsu, Kaneshige, Mitsuhira and Yasusada, made robust yet elegant weapons. Many of these swords commissioned for samurai bear on the tangs the appraisal records of the Yamano family of sword testers, who for a fee would test a sword at the execution ground on the body of a condemned criminal, or on a substitute straw dummy.

On the other hand, the second largest city, Osaka, was populated almost entirely by merchants, who were allowed to carry a single short sword. As the merchants became richer and the samurai became poorer, the merchants' taste for decorative blades with pretty engravings came to dictate style to the smiths. For this reason the majority of swords of the period were *wakizashi* with picturesque *hamon*. Among the better smiths were Sukehiro and his pupil Sukenao, who contrived the *toran* ('billowing') *hamon* in the form of the billowing waves of the sea. Yoshimichi of Tamba made the *sudareba hamon* in imitation of the hanging bamboo curtain, and other smiths represented mountains, flowers and other such untraditional and unwarlike motifs. Carvings on sword blades had always shown the religious awareness, martial spirit, or confidence of the samurai, but from the middle of the Edo period they became a matter of pure decoration. Images of gods of wealth rather than those of war were carved on the blades.

A nationalist and revivalist movement seeking to recall the warlike spirit of the Middle Ages arose towards the end of the eighteenth century against a political background of opposition to the Tokugawas' policies of peace and exclusion and of a desire to restore the 'puppet' emperors to full Imperial power. This nationalistic movement was partially inspired by an awareness of the might and technological superiority of the navies of Russia and other countries. These feelings led artists and craftsmen to explore the styles and techniques of much earlier periods and to try to copy or revive them. This happened, for example, to the sword-makers under the guiding light of Suishinshi Masahide, who began to study old styles of forging and visited provincial smiths to learn the secrets of their ancestors. Among his pupils Naotane was pre-eminent, making blades in the manner of the Sōshū and Bizen smiths. Swords made in this new spirit are called *shinshintō* ('new new swords') and are increasingly admired today.

By the nineteenth century great numbers of long, broad swords were being made. It was, in effect, an attempt to reverse the trend during the Momoyama period when swords were cut down to a shorter length for convenience. These revivalist swords were fearsome-looking weapons:

From left to right

19A. Sword blade with two grooves. *Hamon* of 'wild' *nie*. Signed 'Made by Fujiwara Kunisada resident in Mushū province'. Horikawa school, early 17th century. L. excluding tang 71.3 cm.

19B. Sword blade. *Hamon* of 'billowing' *nie*. Signed 'Sukenao, lord of Omi, living in Takagi'. Osaka work, late 17th century. L. excluding tang 71.2 cm.

19C. Sword blade with a single groove and a narrow following groove. *Hamon* of 'clove flower' *nioi*. Signed 'Made by Enju Nobukatsu'. Dated equivalent to 1844. L. excluding tang 80 cm.

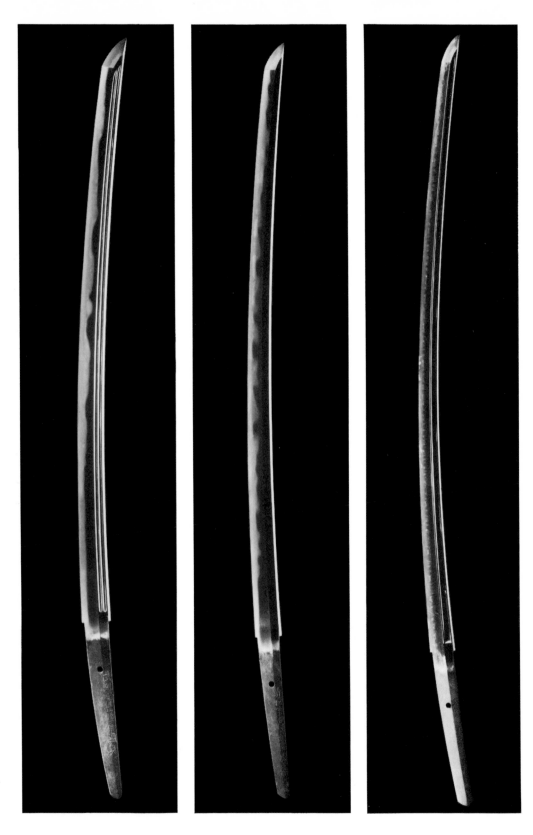

particularly impressive were the works of Kiyomaro in Sōshū style, while good new smiths emerged in Edo, Osaka, Satsuma and Bizen.

Many of the *shinshintō*, however, were inelegant, and the steel lacked the beauty of both the established Edo-period traditions and the old schools. Most poor-quality swords found in Western collections are of this sort, with a heavy shape and a dull surface. The majority of swords used by Japanese forces in the Second World War were an outcome of this debased style.

The metal mountings of the sword included items in iron, especially the guards which were quite frequently of this material. These are discussed together in the following section under precious metals and their alloys.

Precious metals and their alloys

Ieyasu, the first shogun, had appropriated the immense gold and silver holdings of his predecessor Hideyoshi and he further laid claim to all mines and mining rights in Japan, including copper. A system of licensing and government inspectorates was established, yet there was some illicit mining in remote provinces. Copper became very important as it was Japan's most valuable export in return for which she imported sugar, foreign silks and many luxuries from abroad. Most of the ore was mined in North-west Japan, notably Sado Island.

Both silver and gold were used in the pure state, or in alloy for decorating metalwork, in powder form for use with lacquer (p. 80), and as foil for religious and architectural decoration or for the preparation of the gold and silver background of painted screens. They were also used for currency, and various debased forms of bullion were produced. Both were also alloyed with copper to give a variety of metals, all of which could be pickled to give an extraordinary range of coloured patinas. Perhaps the most 'Japanese' of the alloys was *shakudō*, which contained copper (95–99 per cent), gold (1–5 per cent) and small amounts of silver, antimony and arsenic, sometimes with traces of lead. The alloy was pickled to give a lasting black finish like lacquer, likened during the Muromachi period to the colour of a wet crow's wing; but the various forms of the alloy could also present shades of brown, blue and purple.

Shibuichi (or *rōgin*) was an alloy of silver with copper which could be polished white but which was usually presented in various shades of grey. *Shibuichi* (literally, 'one part in four') contained around a quarter silver alloyed with copper, but there was a white form which contained more silver and a dark form which contained *shakudō* in the ratio of about seven parts to three of silver. The addition of gold up to about 1 per cent was said to enrich the colour.

The surface texture, often including a patina, is the main feature of all Japanese metalwork, and whereas those on certain dark bronzes and *shakudō* remain fairly constant, others such as the natural blackening of silver were encouraged to develop into a homely maturity which the metalworker had in mind from the moment of his first inspiration for the subject.

Since the main use for all these metals was in the decoration of sword furniture, we must now turn by way of introduction to a description of how the sword was mounted. As the samurai's most prized possession, the sword was the subject of carefully thought-out workmanship. The province and character of a samurai could be told by a glance at his sword.

The samurai's standard *daisho*, or pair of long and short swords, was, with minor variations, always mounted in technically the same way and the same parts are found on both the *katana* (long sword), and the *wakizashi* (short sword). On non-formal occasions both were thrust through the belt (in their scabbards), blade upwards. The scabbard was of magnolia wood, which did not harm the polished steel blade, and was lacquered for strength and appearance; and the hilt was also of wood, covered in ray skin and elaborately bound with silk braid. Each end of the hilt was fitted with a metal piece: the *fuchi* (collar) fitted around the hilt just above the guard, and the *kashira* (the butt) covered the end. A small decorative piece (*menuki*) under the binding on either side aided the grip on the hilt. The blade was kept tight in the scabbard by a copper collar, or *habaki*. The chape of the scabbard, or *kojiri*, was sometimes of horn and sometimes of metal. The *kurikata* (literally, 'chestnut shape') was a protrusion on the side of the scabbard which prevented it from slipping through the belt and allowed passage of the *sageo* (carrying cord). The *kaeshizuno*, a further protrusion lower down on the scabbard, prevented the scabbard from travelling upwards through the belt.

The scabbard could have up to two slots which held the *kogatana* (utility knife) and *kōgai* (bodkin). These projected slightly beyond the hilt in the direction of the scabbard. Consequently, when they were to be used, the *tsuba* had to include apertures for them as well as the central aperture through which the tang of the sword had to slide. The *tsuba*, or sword-guard, was perhaps the most striking part of the mounting and varied from being a simple iron disk to a graphic display of coloured metal inlays and encrustations.

The ancient *tachi* style mounting, for use with armour and on certain formal occasions, was similar except that the hilt was not always bound and was carried suspended by braid cords from the belt instead of thrust through it. Metal bands on the scabbard which carried the suspending cords were called *ashi-kanamono* and a reinforcing band a third of the way along the scabbard was called the *semegane*. There was also a form of

20. *Wakizashi* mounting, the scabbard of black lacquer and the fittings *shakudō* with gold inlay. Mino school, 17th century. Overall L. 47 cm.

mounting known as *aikuchi*, found mainly on daggers, which had no *tsuba*, so that the *fuchi* abutted a metal rim on the mouth of the scabbard.

The development of taste in sword furniture can be shown by discussing some significant broad groupings of styles of decoration under the various types of fitting. It must be emphasised that the range of size and shape of any of these fittings was strictly limited by convention and practicality, and the decorative metalworker had to exercise great ingenuity in providing varied and interesting designs within those limitations. During the early period iron *tsuba*, decorated with bold inlay, of the several schools of Higo Province in Kyūshū, such as Shimizu, Nishigaki, Hirata and Hayashi, were favoured by the samurai for their simple strength of design. Typical of this group was the 'Shingen' *tsuba*, named after the general Takeda Shingen, which was a sound iron plate inlaid with copper or brass wire sometimes in the form of a continuous stylised centipede.

Another major style also from Kyūshū was displayed in *namban tsuba*, which are said to have first been copied from Chinese imports and possibly manufactured by the Chinese at Nagasaki. The work consisted of elaborately carved iron open-work in interlaced patterns incorporating Chinese symbols and small amounts of gold overlay. A major difference from all other styles of *tsuba* is that the iron was liable to rust away, whereas most pure Japanese ironwork was given a stable black or brown patina. Plain iron *tsuba* were always in demand, and several schools specialised in designs in both negative and positive silhouettes pierced through the iron plate.

Associated with the swordsmith Yasutsugu and the Shimosaka school in Echizen were a number of makers of carved iron *tsuba*. They included the Myōchin, Akao and Nagasone, but the best known were the carvers who signed themselves Kinai. These metalworkers made bold designs in roundly carved and pierced hard black iron. They were especially skilful in depicting dragons, on *tsuba* and also carved deep into the blades of swords.

Swordsmiths and armour-makers also made *tsuba*. Those made by swordsmiths tended to be only of practical use and are not of any artistic merit; their work is mostly unsigned with some exceptions like that of Okisato Kotetsu, who had originally been an armourer. Signed pieces usually date from the late eighteenth to the mid-nineteenth centuries, when simple pierced designs in keeping with the revivalist sword-making movement were made in considerable numbers. Armourers' work of the early period is sometimes characterised by designs which are based on the shapes of armour itself.

In Kyoto the brilliant metalworker of the Momoyama period, Umetada Myōjū, made *tsuba* of lively and coloured flat inlaid designs on copper alloys. His designs are indicative of the joy in nature of the inhabitants of Kyoto and the extrovert yet sure sense of design traditional in the ancient capital. Other makers worked in this rather unmilitary manner in the early period, to blossom out in the late seventeenth century into the *machibori* schools of pure decoration (p. 42).

Formal scabbards of samurai when resident in Edo had to be black, and at least the *fuchi* and *menuki* of the hilt had to be made in Gotō style. The Gotō family had served in turn the Ashikaga shoguns in the fifteenth century, then Hideyoshi and finally the Tokugawas. Branches of the

21. *Tsuba* pierced and carved in the form of a coiled dragon. Patinated iron. Signed 'Made by Kinai living in Echizen'. 17th century. 7.6 × 7.4 cm.

22. *Tsuba*, decorated with flowers and a horse, in gold inlay on a *nanako* ground in *skakudō*. Mino school, 17th century. 6.7 × 7.1 cm.

school worked for the provincial *daimyō*, although the main branch worked in Edo. Their work is known as *iebori*, or 'house carving', because they were sponsored by the ruling house. Their fittings were at first limited to *menuki*, *kozuka* and *kōgai* but they later came to make *tsuba* and all the other pieces. Gotō sword-fittings were invariably made of *shakudō* with inlaid and overlaid decoration in gold. Their speciality was the form of prepared ground known as *nanako* (fish roe), which consisted of arrays of small regular protruberances formed on the *shakudō* with a hollow punch.

Themes of the Gotō school were taken frequently from Chinese legend and represented *shishi*, dragons, *kirin* (griffins), birds, flowers and objects related to the intellectual pursuits of the shoguns such as the *Nō* theatre, the Tea Ceremony and music. Much of the work incorporated inlaid *mon* for use on the formal sword mounting.

The emphasis on preserving the official style led to the Gotō work becoming over-formalised and unimaginative, so that the richer samurai on informal occasions and the merchants came to seek more ostentatious fittings. By the early eighteenth century, therefore, the Gotō school had become overshadowed by the independent studios of the *machibori* ('town carving') artists, among whose unconfined works is found the true expression of the Japanese imagination in the metalwork medium. Yokoya Sōmin (1670–1733), perhaps the originator and certainly one of the greatest of the *machibori* artists, had actually been schooled in the Gotō tradition; but his artistic temperament led him away from the school, and he turned to the production of crowded and lively human scenes in high-relief work dressed with a greater range of coloured metals than the Gotōs

23. *Tsuba* with a Buddhist guardian king clasping a *vajra* (thunderbolt). Brass with copper, *shakudō* and gold high-relief inlay. Signed Ichiryūken Tomonobu. 19th century. 7.8 × 8.6 cm.

24. *Tsuba* carved with a flock of plovers in *shibuichi*. Signed Hirochika. 19th century. 5.8 × 6.4 cm.

42

allowed. He is credited with developing the art of engraving with oblique chisel cuts in simulation of brushwork.

It is among the schools of *machibori* artists that the greatest of Japanese decorative metalworkers, such as the Ōmori, Yanagawa, Kikuoki, Hamano and Ishiguro, are found. The three great artists of Nara, Toshinaga, Jōi and Yasuchika, were especially notable for their lively designs and techniques which made wide use of the natural world of Japan – landscapes, flowers and birds, and picturesque objects such as tea bowls and fans. Towards the end of the nineteenth century, when swords were banned except for the armed forces, the pupils of the Gotō master Ichijō himself introduced many innovations in design and extended their work to objects other than sword furniture. Ichijō and Kanō Natsuō were the last great masters of decorative metalwork in direct contact with the traditions of the samurai sword.

After the emergence of the *machibori* schools, the same artists made *tsuba*, *fuchi-kashira* and other fittings in soft metals. They were usually made in matching pairs, either with similar designs or with complementary narrative material. The early *fuchi-kashira* were simple pieces and very often robustly constructed of iron, although the Mino, Gotō and some other artists produced soft-metal decorative pieces.

The *kozuka* was the hilt of the small utility knife which fitted into the hilt of the scabbard, and the makers were different from those who made the blades. It was made either of a single sheet folded and joined along one edge or a decorative plate set into a box-like frame to allow insertion of the blade. In some cases plates of *nanako* provided by specialist *nanako*-makers

25. *Fuchi-kashira* set with the immortals Gamma Sennin (with the toad) and Tekkai Sennin (exhaling his spirit). *Shakudō* with copper, *shakudō* and gold inlays on a *nanako* ground. Signed Eishō. Second quarter of 18th century. L. (*fuchi*) 3.4 cm; L. (*kashira*) 3.7 cm.

43

26. Pair of *menuki* in the form of the Buddhist guardian kings Tamonten and Zōchōten. Copper with gold overlay. 18th or 19th century. H. 4.7 cm.

were decorated with small carved pieces fixed on with rivets. The blades of *kozuka* often bore apocryphal inscriptions of the names of great swordsmiths, but some really were the work of swordsmiths and had forging grain and *hamon*, like swords. The *kōgai* were general-purpose bodkins, very similar in shape to the Japanese hairpin, which seem to have originated either as a pin for fixing the helmet to the hair, or as an identifying marker which could be left in the body of a vanquished foe. The samurai of Higo Province carried a thick form of *kōgai* called a *bashin*, which was used for letting the blood of horses; but generally the *kōgai* of the Edo period seems to have been merely a personal accessory and possibly mainly used for cleaning the ears by means of the lip at the end. Some *kōgai* split into two to form chopsticks known as *waribashi*.

Menuki were originally the heads of pins which secured the tang of the blade into the hilt and were not strikingly ornate. With the development of binding the hilt with silk braid, however, they came to be regarded as important items of sword furniture. As they were small and usually hollowed out, some skill in repoussé work was required to make good *menuki*, and not every *tsuba* artist could attempt it.

Two *menuki* were used, usually in matching pairs of the same or very similar subjects, one either side of the hilt. The one visible on the outside when the sword was worn indicated *yo* (yang – the male principle), and the other *in* (yin – the female principle). They were arranged to coincide with the position of the hands when the sword was held with the right hand near the *tsuba* and the left hand near the butt. *Menuki* were thus set sometimes to be gripped inside the fingers; although the Yagyū school of swordsmanship to the Tokugawa government specified that they should be the other way round, and other schools of fencing required them to occupy the space between the hands.

Although their main market was for sword furniture, the early *machibori* artists had made netsuke and other ornamental metalwork, but towards the end of the Edo period they branched out into the manufacture of all kinds of decorative work.

The bowls and mouthpieces of pipes were generally of metal and the stem was of wood. Generally the metal parts were of simple copper, gilt, silvered or brass, but late nineteenth-century work was often quite ornate with much repoussé decoration. A set of pipe and tobacco pouch was carried suspended from the belt, and sometimes a metal ashtray in a hemispherical shape would hang with them and double as the retaining toggle (netsuke). The bowls of Japanese pipes are very small, allowing only a few puffs, and the ashtray netsuke is said to have been used to hold the glowing embers from which the next pipeful was lit.

Netsuke in the form of cast or carved models of objects, creatures or people in the round were a new challenge to the metalworkers. The skills of sword-furniture makers were largely in engraving and inlay on prepared surfaces, and for this reason and because of the uncomfortable weight of such pieces the majority of good metal netsuke are of the *kagami-buta* ('mirror-plate') type. This consisted of a decorative disk of metal set into a case of wood or ivory. Artists such as Kōmin, Shōmin and Natsuō produced these during the last decades of the nineteenth century, when they seem to have been much admired by Western visitors and collectors.

44

27. (*Left*) *Kozuka* with two
crows perched on a branch
against the moon. *Shibuichi*
with silver and *skakudō*
inlay. Signed Rinsendō
Mitsuyoshi. 19th century.
L. 9 cm; (*right*) *kozuka* with a
wood-grain pattern formed
by two different copper
alloys. Signed Yoshitoshi.
19th century. L. 9 cm.

One may even find sets of these little round plates in fitted velvet boxes made in Japan at this period for sale to Westerners. (For netsuke see Chapter 3.)

The cords by which a tobacco pouch or similar object hung from the sash were drawn together through a small bead known as an *ojime*, which was often made of metal. The repoussé method was used to make two hollowed-out halves and to create the surface designs themselves. The two halves were soldered together to form a sphere or lozenge, often so cunningly that the joint remains invisible except under strong magnification. In the late nineteenth century these *ojime* became almost a miniature metal art form in themselves, and many seem to have been made with an eye to the tastes of Western visitors. Indeed, some were strung as necklaces in Western style. Kanō Natsuō was perhaps the greatest master of this most miniature of Japanese arts.

The techniques used in *menuki* were adopted increasingly during the Edo period for fittings for leather and brocade purses and pouches, lacquer boxes and other everyday objects. These fittings are known as *kanamono* ('metal things'). They are often bigger than *menuki*, of square or oblong shape, and have metal pins at the back to fix into the leather or other surface. Like *menuki* they were frequently produced in pairs (4B). In the second half of the nineteenth century major makers such as the Myōchin, Shōami and Gotō groups were signing pieces of this sort.

In this period too the brilliant techniques of the Japanese metalworker were applied to an ever-increasing range of objects, both useful and bizarre, for export to the Western world where they still abound.

28. (*Right*) Pouch-fitting with the theme of 'the old man of Takasago' with a huge dish of saké and an auspicious turtle. *Shibuichi* with applied copper, *shakudō*, silver and gold in high relief. Signed Kōmin. Late 19th century. 2.9 × 2.4 cm.

29. (*Opposite*) Ornamental vase decorated with a flowering cherry-tree and a figure carrying brushwood. Red patinated copper with copper, *shakudō*, silver and gold inlay. Inscribed 'Made in Japan'. Late 19th century. H. 23.5 cm.

46

47

30. Lantern clock with a single
foliot. Iron working in iron case
inlaid with silver and gold.
Dated equivalent to 1678.
36 × 13.5 × 13.5 cm.

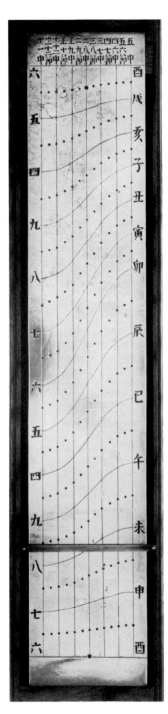

31. The face of a pillar clock, showing by means of a graph the variation in the length of hours due to the seasons. The characters on the right represent the zodiac, and the characters on the left are the equivalent numerals; at the top are six months of the year. Brass. 19th century. 4.5 × 24.3 cm.

Clocks

Although timepieces in the form of candle clocks, water clocks and sundials had been used in Japan for some centuries, the true clockwork mechanism was unknown until the sixteenth century when it was introduced from Europe. There were three basic types of clock used with little change of form and mechanism during the Edo period: the lantern clock, so named because of its similarity to the Japanese lantern with its dome-shaped bell on top; the pillow clock, which resembled the hard Japanese pillow and forms of which were also known as bracket clocks; and the pillar clock, which was of a long vertical narrow format and fitted on to the wooden pillars of the typical Japanese house. Each of these types was originally driven by travelling weights, but coil-spring drives were introduced later in the Edo period.

Until after the Imperial restoration of 1868, the system of time measurement was according to the ancient Chinese zodiac. The twelve animals of the zodiac in their fixed order represented twelve 'hours' of day and night, divided into six hours of day and six hours of night, in theory from sunrise and sunset. The lengths of the hours of both day and night thus varied according to the season. The signs for the 'hours' were shown on clock dials with the sign of the horse at the position of midday in the clockwise order shown below. The numeral attached to each sign indicates the number of chimes struck, which have no arithmetical relationship with the number of the hour itself.

HORSE, 9 (noon); GOAT, 8; APE, 7; COCK, 6; DOG, 5; BOAR, 4;
RAT, 9 (midnight); BULL, 8; TIGER, 7; HARE, 6; DRAGON, 5; SERPENT, 4;

Several ingenious devices were developed to compensate for the variation in the length of the 'hours'. An early method was to provide means for changing manually the positions of two weights on the single foliot at sunset and sunrise, thus altering its effective length. Another method for circular-dial clocks was to replace the single moving hour hand with a fixed hand and to connect a moving dial into which sliding plates representing the hours were fixed. The clock could then be run at a single speed both night and day, and the proportion of the circle appropriate to night and day simply altered. Some such dials have black *shakudō* plates for night and white silver plates for day. A later more advanced device was the provision of a double foliot, with a mechanism for automatically switching from one to the other at sunrise and sunset.

The pillar clocks indicated time by a pointer which travelled in a vertical straight line past metal hour plates which could easily be adjusted by hand. These were numbered from four to nine as described above. A later development was a changeable programme inscribed on a black-lacquered vertical slat, which would be fitted into the pillar of the clock. These slats allowed for the variations in the length of hours in any specified period of ten days in the year. A still later and more sophisticated programme provided vertical parallel markings indicating the seasons, with the variation in length of hours shown by curved lines crossing these season lines, so that the time during any of the fixed ten-day periods could be read by looking where the horizontal travelling pointer crossed the appropriate season line. This device amply demonstrates the skill of the Japanese in mathematics during the period of Isolation.

Some clocks also incorporated calendars with the twelve signs of the zodiac and the five pairs of 'elemental' signs displayed through their sixty combinations, which in their fixed order represent a continuously running cycle of sixty years, months, days, hours or even seconds.

Currency

The political system imposed by Ieyasu, the first Tokugawa shogun, had as great an impact on Japan's currency as it did on the nation's other institutions. Before the Edo period the monetary system was based on the use of precious metals by weight and imported Chinese cast-bronze coins or their local imitations. Ieyasu organised these two elements into a centralised coinage system which his successors maintained with diminishing degrees of success until the Meiji Restoration.

From 1626 the official bronze coinage was of only one permitted type, based on the Chinese coins in shape and design but inscribed *Kan'ei Tsuho*, 'circulating Treasure of the Kan'ei era'. They were first cast in the third year of the Kan'ei era (1626). Numerous mints were set up to cast these coins in vast quantities so that the whole nation would be able to use them as the principal medium for everyday trade. For larger transactions Ieyasu systematised the use of precious metals by setting up mints to manufacture gold and silver coins based respectively on the ingot currencies of the Edo and Kyoto areas. His gold coins were flat ovals or rectangles marked with authorising stamps and denominated by weight. The silver coins were crude slugs or beans, also marked with authorising stamps but of variable weight. The local preferences in Edo for gold coins and in Kyoto for silver persisted, but both were legal tender throughout Japan.

The successors of Ieyasu attempted to maintain a currency based on his reforms until the end of the shogunate; they were not able to adhere to the standards he established. The political stability of the shogunate encouraged trade, but the mints could not keep up with the demand for coinage this stimulated. Initially many of the pre-Edo-period local ingot currencies and imported cash inconveniently survived in circulation, but by the 1660s sufficient official coin was in use to enable the shogun to proscribe the earliest issues successfully by edict. However, in the mean time the mercantile community created a far worse impediment to the official coinage by introducing the use of paper currency as a substitute for precious metal coins. This practice spread rapidly so that many feudal lords also issued paper money. The shoguns tried to ban this practice and succeeded in suppressing it temporarily from 1707 until 1730. Although they occasionally tried to ban it again at later dates, from 1730 the quantity of locally produced paper money continued to grow until over 300 different issuing authorities had placed notes into circulation. In spite of this the shoguns continued the issue of coins; however, inflation caused by the paper money and an ever-increasing demand for coinage led them progressively to debase the precious metal coins and in 1740 to issue iron coins in the place of bronze so that monetary activities could continue.

Towards the end of Tokugawa rule there were attempts to consolidate the coinage by issuing new silver coins denominated in relation to the gold

32. Gold Ōban 10 *ryō* coin issued in 1725; inscribed in ink with its weight and the signature of the controller of the gold mint and stamped with the Tokugawas' authorising marks. 15.4 × 9.5 cm.

coins and token bronze coins, but the system had already degenerated too far. The massive exports of gold (which the Japanese undervalued in relation to silver) that followed the opening of Japanese ports to foreign trade led to its final collapse along with that of the shogunate. While the last Tokugawas struggled to control the situation with a fresh reform in 1860, some of the more powerful feudal lords were able to protect themselves from the resulting chaos by issuing their own local silver coins, or base metal tokens. This situation survived the shogunate by two years when in 1870 the Meiji emperor reformed the currency along the lines of a European coinage and gradually withdrew from circulation the local paper currency and the debased gold, silver and iron coins, the meagre remains of Ieyasu's currency system.

3

SCULPTURE AND DECORATIVE CARVING

Neither in Japan nor in the West would one normally expect a chapter on sculpture to be included in a book on decorative arts. However, in the period 1600–1900 it is a curious fact that much Japanese natural talent for the plastic arts (carving, moulding and engraving) was expressed in forms which cannot be considered large-scale sculpture and were with very few exceptions either light-hearted or simply decorative.

In Chaper 1 we discussed the Japanese craftsman's high status which included a degree of semi-religious respect, especially in certain ancient and highly esteemed crafts. That respect came originally from the attitudes of the native Shintō religion, although Shintō almost never represented its gods in major images to be worshipped; it was rather in the Buddhist religion, introduced during the sixth century AD, that sculpture came to be considered a major art together with painting, calligraphy and, of course, the building of temples themselves, and Buddhism, eager in its early missionary period not to be outdone by the native Shintō respect for skill, was quick to bestow its own titles on craftsmen who worked for it. Of these the title *Busshi* ('Buddhist Master') was used from the earliest historical period of Japanese art and was applied to sculptors. In the eleventh century the more exalted terms of *Hōgan*, *Hokkyō* and *Hōin* ('Eye of the Law', 'Bridge of the Law' and 'Seal of the Law') were given to Buddhist sculptors and painters. By the Edo period these titles had become

33. Buddhist priest in meditation.
Painted wood. 17th century.
H. 40.5 cm.

52

bestowable, in return for some sort of work or consideration, on almost any artist or craftsman, and the practice was much abused until all such titles were abolished in 1873.

Buddhism offered the only scope for large-scale sculpture in traditional Japan. There was no place for major architectural sculpture in the austere style of building described in Chapter 1, and there was no monumental sculpture of political figures. Great men, like Ieyasu himself, were commemorated in Shintō shrines devoted to them after death when, like all the dead, they became *kami* ('gods'); these shrines rarely included sculptural images, and never large ones. There was no place at all in the grandest Japanese mansions for large sculptures for pleasure such as stood around in the great houses of Europe. Buddhism, then, with its great temple images of Buddhas, Bodhisattvas and attendant divinities, such as the ferocious guardians of the four directions, was the only patron for sculpture as we know it.

However, the great days of traditional Buddhist sculpture had begun to come to an end long before the year 1600, when Ieyasu came to power and ensured beyond any doubt that the Buddhist sects would never again have the political and military power they had enjoyed in the early sixteenth century. For the long civil wars ending in 1600 destroyed many of the great works of the past, disrupted the settled life of monasteries and their craftsmen, and saw a decline in the fervour of belief in a transcendent existence as the major sects became more and more immersed in the brutality of power politics. Even more effective was the decline in wealth of the monasteries. In the Edo period they controlled less land than before, and they were not permitted by the government, in common with the rest of the populace, to indulge in conspicuous consumption. The lack of sectarian fervour and the more worldly spirit of Edo urban society also naturally diminished their contributions.

Yet the crafts of Buddhism had an ancient tradition that remained remarkably persistent, and in Kyoto and Nara especially the old workshops continued to replace and repair the sculptures of the old temples. They produced much new work too in the old style, but it lacked conviction, and quality was clearly affected by shortage of temple funds. Obviously a sculptor of energy and imagination could not be satisfied by such work.

Fortunately, there was a new field for such craftsmen – that of private devotion – which continued or even increased as the Buddhist institutions themselves lost prestige. It took two forms – one a market for small devotional images for use in private houses, or even for carrying about; the other for more conventional images given by individuals to temples by which means they hoped to accumulate virtue for themselves and their families.

Commissions of this sort produced much excellent small sculpture in the Edo period, but the secular, more human temper of the age had a very marked effect on where that excellence was expressed. As a general tendency, it can be said that the older-styled Buddhist images of non-human beings lack force and personality in this period. A typical example is the small bronze standing figure of the Buddha Amida (34) which is dated 1690, at the height of the brilliantly worldly Genroku era, and made at the request of a townsman called Toda. Technically excellent, its

34. The Buddha Amida standing on a lotus pedestal. Gilt bronze. Dated equivalent to 1690. H. 36 cm.

55

blandness speaks for itself. Images, on the other hand, of recognisably human personalities – patriarchs, saints and the historical Buddha during his earthly life – are often vigorous, exciting and passionate. A splendid example, dated 1637, is the seated, meditating bronze figure of the historical Buddha, made by Masakatsu for the Mankōji Temple in Kanazawa (35).

These two pieces are bronzes cast by the lost-wax process (see p. 24) but they are nevertheless sculpture, for the shaping and carving took place at an earlier stage when the wax base was made from which the moulds were created. Moulding of shapes for surface decoration was a persistent but almost unnoticed form of sculpture during this period; it contributed, among many others, to the making of bronze mirrors and iron kettles (see pp. 26–7), of ink-cakes and of porcelain and pottery figures.

Direct carving of wood, nevertheless, remained the preferred medium of the Japanese sculptor. As we have seen in Chapter 1, stone was little used, and except for fairly simple stone lanterns in gardens and courtyards the Japanese world of the Edo period saw stone sculpture only in crude wayside figures of the protective Bodhisattva Jizō or of phallic folk-images which go back even further than Shintō into Japan's past; or in similarly unsophisticated stone Buddhas and Bodhisattvas in graveyards. In wood, though, very accomplished work was done throughout the three centuries under discussion.

A remarkably lifelike example of wood sculpture, datable in style to the seventeenth century, is the seated figure of a Buddhist priest in meditation (33). Although the subject has not been positively identified, the sculptor was clearly working on an unpretentiously human scale and avoided, in typically Edo period style, investing his figure with any sense of the super-human. Yet it would be a mistake to assume that he was necessarily working from life. Miwa's portrait of Sesshū (36), made in 1788, is full of a feeling of presence, but it is in fact an imaginative reconstruction of a personality of three centuries earlier based on a painting. By ancient practice the great were portrayed only posthumously; any such portrait, whether painted or sculpted, was therefore from a combination of memory and tradition.

The seated priest was made using the *yosegi* technique which was developed in the eleventh century to escape from the constraints of the single block of wood. It consisted of hollow-carving many parts separately, and then fixing them together and covering the joins with a pigmented surface. The Edo period valued a naturalistic appearance, and this figure has been very carefully and durably finished to that end. It is, in fact, more carefully done than most Buddhist temple sculpture, and the finish is finer and harder than on the masks of the *Nō* drama. Over the wood has been applied a cloth layer soaked in lacquer as a primer, followed by many layers of shell white, then by layers of pigment and a varnish of carefully polished transparent lacquer. On the black outer robe designs of dragons and clouds have been further built up with gesso.

Lifelike glossy surfaces like these were encouraged by the impact of European sculptured images, mainly religious ones, imported by the Portuguese and Spaniards in the second half of the sixteenth century and the first quarter of the seventeenth. The model of a Portuguese trumpeter

35. The Buddha meditating after ascetic practices, by Masakatsu. Gilt bronze. Dated equivalent to 1637. H. 34.6 cm.

36. The artist Sesshū (1420–1506) as a priest, by Miwa. Various hardwoods. Dated equivalent to 1788. H. 23.5 cm.

37. A Portuguese trumpeter. Painted wood. c. 1600. H. 26.5 cm.

(37) is a rare example of a piece of carving for sheer amusement with no apparent function. It dates from around 1600 and uses similar techniques of pigmentation. In the third quarter of the eighteenth century Yoshimura Shūzan (died 1776) became famous for the similarly fine and durable pigments he applied to carved netsuke, which were widely copied for a century afterwards. The difficulty of achieving durability with attractive pigments is proved by the fact that most netsuke of this sort have in fact lost their colours through use.

For this reason, as well as on account of the more restrained side of Japanese taste which held natural materials in high esteem, most small and miniature sculptures and other objects carved into sculptural shapes were left in natural wood, bamboo or ivory, or simply stained. This was even true of netsuke carved in the shape of miniature masks, although the original full-sized masks were always coloured. Masks persisted as a form of minor sculpture through the Edo period. Widely used for Buddhist and Shintō festivals, as well as for ordinary street dances, their forms were traditional. So, too, were the masks for the two more formal types of entertainment, *Bugaku* and *Nō*, for which the product had to be rather more sophisticated.

58

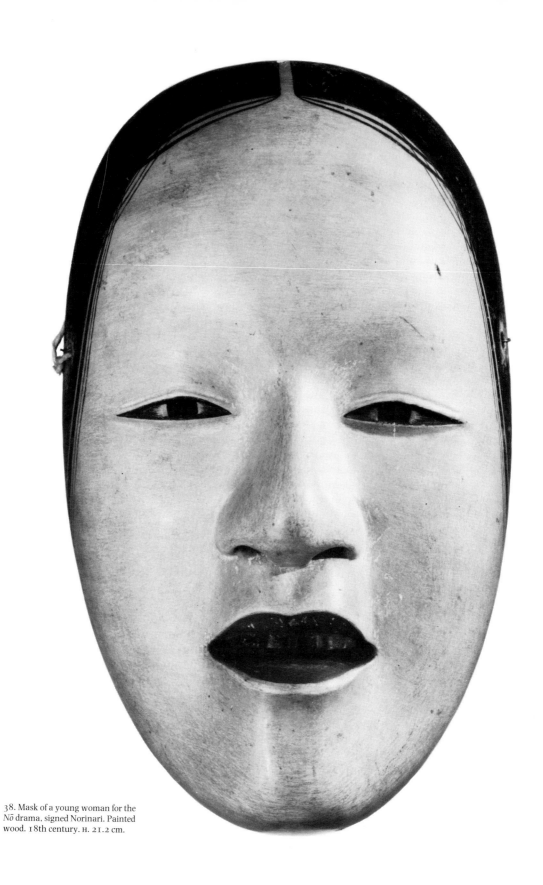

38. Mask of a young woman for the
Nō drama, signed Norinari. Painted
wood. 18th century. H. 21.2 cm.

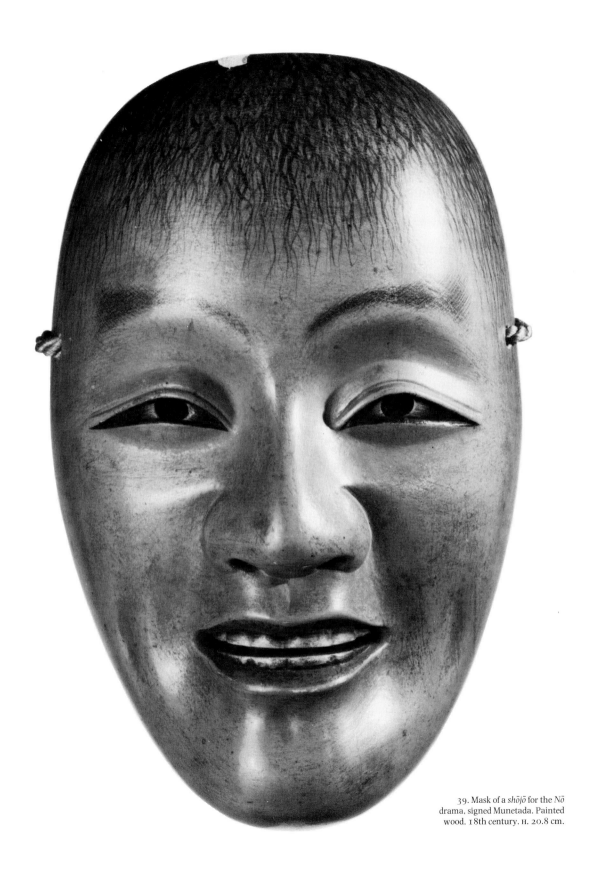

39. Mask of a *shōjō* for the *Nō* drama, signed Munetada. Painted wood. 18th century. H. 20.8 cm.

Bugaku was a colourful dance-drama originating in the ninth century and flourishing up to the twelfth century as a courtly entertainment with elaborate rules, steps and music. Tokugawa Ieyasu re-established it with government support in Edo and Kyoto, and the study of ancient masks led to a vigorous revival of the art. The illustration in colour (6) shows just such a mask, used for the character Ryō-Ō – a victorious Chinese warrior aided by a dragon, who appears on the head. In *Bugaku* the characters are grotesque, mythical and of continental rather than Japanese origin; their features are jutting and often ferocious. The detachable chin and the free-moving eyes are typical *Bugaku* features, allowing those parts to move with the rhythm of the dance. The extremely good technique of the carving and pigmentation of Edo-period *Bugaku* masks makes them sometimes hard to distinguish from those of the Heian and Kamakura periods.

Greater subtlety was required of a *Nō* mask because it did not cover the front of the head as in *Bugaku* but hid only the face itself. The *Nō* drama was an entirely Japanese invention, having originated and flourished in the fourteenth and fifteenth centuries under the patronage of the Ashikaga shoguns in Kyoto. Ieyasu decided to place it under his protection, and different schools of acting settled in Kyoto and Edo for the edification of the samurai class, to whom the performances were mainly restricted (though there were sometimes benefit and gala performances for the ordinary people).

Nō was poetic, musical, dramatic, intensely slow and yet visually brilliant, at least as far as the principal actors were concerned. They wore magnificent brocaded robes of great presence, and the masks had to be strong enough to stand up to that competition. At the same time they had to be subtle enough to reflect the delicate emotions put into the performance by the actor and to give him scope to do that. Because of this delicate balance, which put the mask carver under severe restrictions, a tradition soon developed that masks should represent the *types* of person (human or non-human) who appeared in the plays.

The commonest type was the 'young woman' mask, which like others did in fact have variants for the different schools of acting, each patronising their favoured schools of carvers working in Japan during the Edo period. In spite of its apparent standardisation, it is surprising what subtleties of feeling carvers succeeded in putting into this image. In Illustration 38 the maker has achieved a sense of agonised strain beneath what seems a slight smile. He uses the traditional made-up face of the court lady, which had not much changed since the Heian period and which was still the ideal of female beauty. The straight, long black hair is divided in the centre of the forehead, with a few artfully arranged strands standing out over the dead-white face make-up. The eyebrows are painted out and then painted in again high up on the forehead. The lips are reddened, and the teeth blackened.

This is as much a triumph of painting as of carving, but there is no evidence that the work was divided among more than one person. Certainly contemporary *Nō* mask carvers do all the processes themselves. A less remote treatment can be seen in the mask of a *shōjō* (39), a mythical half-human creature always red-faced from drinking saké, which appears in relatively few plays. Here the tousled hair is painted in with a delicate brush over the orange-red skin. The absence of make-up reaching to the very edges of the eyes has allowed the maker more freedom in carving.

Even more freedom was allowed when making masks of demons and completely mythical creatures. When mask carvers turned to making netsuke to improve their standard of living, it was these demonic masks which were the most popular. Illustration 40 shows a large netsuke of the mask of Hannya, used for several *Nō* parts in which a jealous, passionate

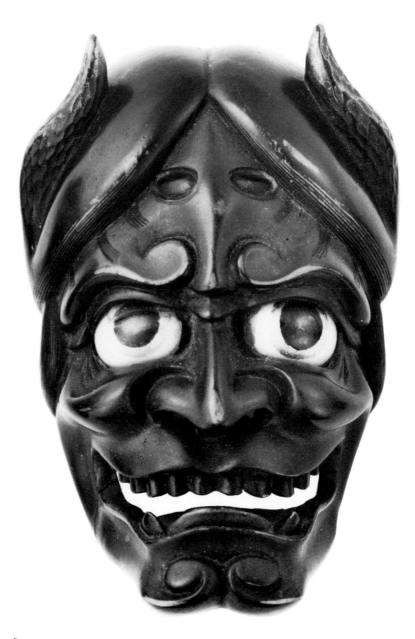

40. Netsuke mask of the demon Hannya, signed Deme Shūzan. Painted wood. Mid-19th century. H. 8.2 cm.

41. The Buddha coming down from the mountains. Wood, formerly painted. 17th or 18th century. H. 31 cm.

42. Miniature shrine with figure of the thousand-armed Kannon and painted images of the gods of wind and thunder. Wood, lacquered and painted, with gilding and bronze fittings. 17th century. H. 16.2 cm.

woman had turned into a vengeful demon. This example is signed by Deme Shūzan, a member of the Edo branch of the Deme family which had made *Nō* masks since the sixteenth century and became the main carvers of mask netsuke. The first Shūzan of this family worked in the late eighteenth century but he had several successors in the early and mid-nineteenth centuries. The large size and fine preservation of this particular example suggest that it is from the later period when netsuke carvers were beginning to break out of the miniature form which constrained them.

Masks were popular in the Edo period because, as representations of faces, they were more human and therefore more easily understandable in human terms. The same taste affected the sculpture of the period, where there is far greater emphasis on the face than on the whole effect. The delightful figure of the historical Buddha in Illustration 41 is relatively conventional in its treatment of robes and limbs but succeeds because of its relaxed, benign and, above all, humane face. In its small size it is a typical piece of the period. On the other hand, the miniature shrine (42) is artistically a failure, in spite of its brilliant technique, because the face of

the Bodhisattva Kannon is blank and inexpressive. More enthusiasm has gone into the painted figures of the gods of wind and thunder which decorate the insides of the doors.

This sort of small shrine was made for private devotion, and the smallest ones could be carried about conveniently by private citizens. Many were made in the seventeenth century. The figure itself is a miracle of miniature carving but can have afforded little satisfaction to the maker, or indeed to the perceptive buyer. It is not surprising, then, that by the late seventeenth century carvers were beginning to seek new forms in which they could better express their energy.

One of these was the netsuke. If we compare a netsuke of a Buddhist Guardian (*Niō*) made in the late eighteenth century with the shrine figure, both being approximately the same size, the difference is strikingly obvious (43). The *Niō* was made in the late eighteenth century by a maker signing his name as Ranrinsai Shūzan. Although the name Shūzan is written with the same characters as the mask carver Deme Shūzan, referred to above, there is no other evidence that they are the same person, since the studio name Ranrinsai is recorded only on this one piece. This splendidly vigorous carving has all the energy of the Buddhist sculpture of earlier periods, when ferocious *Niō* over 5 m high might stand in recesses at each side of the temple gate. At the same time, though, it has humour, and it is this quality of light-heartedness that seems most to have suited the temper of the times and to have released a flood of sculptural activity. There is graphic confirmation of this outlook in a woodblock book called *Shōshoku Ekagami* illustrated by Keisai Masayoshi and published in 1794. The book's title means 'A pictorial mirror of all crafts', and it is in fact a whole series of stock subjects which could be used on almost any decorative object. It includes the two *Niō*, both of which have a slight but undeniable grin.

The joke, of course, in the netsuke version is that the *Niō* is holding in his left hand, instead of the traditional thunderbolt, a tobacco pipe, and in his right a tobacco pouch with a netsuke attached to it. This illustrates nicely the function of a netsuke, which is, in fact, no more than a retaining toggle, used to hold the pouch on its cord in the belt (*obi*) which encircled the waist of almost every type of dress, including that of the samurai. In Illustration 45 a man of samurai class can be seen talking to a carver of *Nō* masks. Instead of a tobacco pouch he has slung through his *obi* a purse made of a dyed textile, held by a netsuke.

This netsuke, and the one worn by the *Niō*, are of the simplest sort known as a *manjū* after a round, dome-shaped rice-cake still eaten in Japan. *Manjū* were more often of ivory than of wood, and they appear most frequently in Edo-period illustrations when the wearing of a netsuke can be identified. As early as 1690 a pictorial encyclopedia called *Jinrin Kimmō Zui* illustrates a worker in ivory, among whose minor products are listed netsuke, which must from the simplicity of the other wares he made be of the *manjū* type. The great majority of netsuke must have been *manjū*, which were easily turned on the lathe, and most were probably undecorated and therefore not treasured or collected. Those found in collections are normally engraved with standard designs, but occasionally they are carved in complete open-work designs of flowers, intertwining dragons, or even mythical scenes (1). This sort of decorative carving,

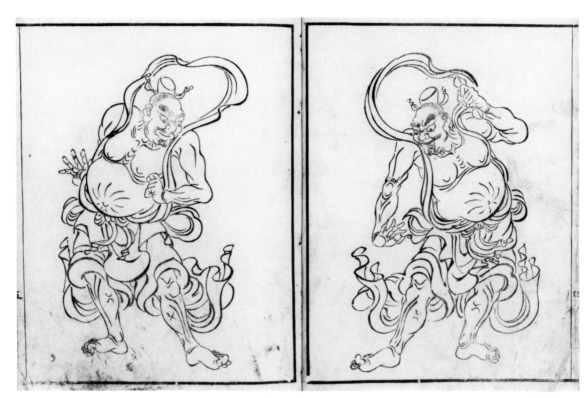

44. *Niō* from the woodblock book *Shōshoku Ekagami*, by Masayoshi, 1794. 252 × 340 mm.

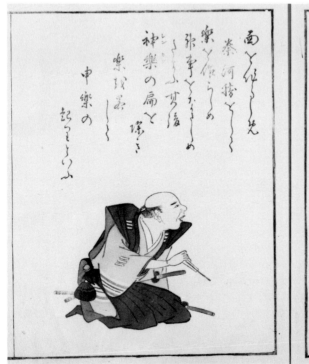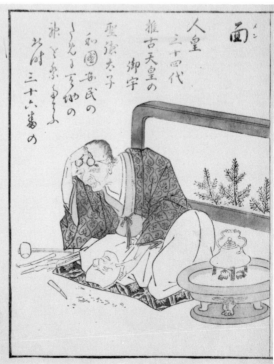

45. A carver of masks with a samurai, from the stencilled book *Saiga Shokunin Burui*, by Minkō, 1770. 285 × 380 mm.

46. (*Above*) Pipe-case carved with a dragon in clouds with tobacco pouch decorated with a lizard, both with brass eyes, and a bead-*ojime* carved with a Buddha. Wood. Early 19th century. L. of pipe-case 27.2 cm.

48. (*Right*) Wrist-rest carved with flowers and pomegranates, signed Kensai. Bamboo. Early 19th century. L. 14.5 cm.

47. (*Above*) Netsuke designs from the woodblock book *Sōken Kishō* by Inaba Tsuryū, 1781. 285 × 220 mm.

whether engraved, in relief, or cut right through, was used on many different types of object, from architectural decoration to pipes, pipe-cases (46), wrist-rests (48), *inrō*, false swords for those not entitled to carry a real weapon, and many other items made of wood, bamboo or ivory. (It should be remembered, though, that all three techniques were also used on decorative metalwork.)

Carving in bamboo is especially difficult because it is so brittle. The Chinese had become masters of this art centuries earlier, but in the eighteenth century the Japanese who aspired to Chinese taste began to encourage bamboo carving which rapidly reached a high level, though it has been little collected in the West with the exception of large brush-pots carved with scenes of geisha, samurai, Mount Fuji and other motifs considered essential by Western purchasers in the late nineteenth century. The wrist-rest, used when handling the brush in calligraphy on a low table, was often made with a section of carved bamboo. The example in Illustration 48 is a fine piece of carving in a characteristic Chinese pattern of entwined fruits, leaves and flowers. Such formal interlacings of plants were very Chinese in flavour and far from the more natural style favoured by pure Japanese taste. The loose trailing of leaves round a bean-pod forming a wooden knife-case by Kaigyokusai (1813–92) shows the difference clearly.

Fully carved netsuke in the round became popular in the first half of the eighteenth century and the earliest are normally in Chinese taste as well. Pictorial evidence suggests that it was the ivory handles of personal seals that were first carved into figures of lion-dogs (*shishi*) or dragons, and that this happened in the second quarter of the eighteenth century when the ban on most Chinese books which had been in operation for some eighty years was relaxed in 1720. Certainly by 1781, when the first discussion of carved netsuke appears in the book *Sōken Kishō*, the majority of them were of mythical Chinese figures. A page from this book in Illustration 47 shows three of this sort – two bearded *Sennin* (Immortals) with staffs; and the 'Demon Queller' Shoki, who was the most popular of them all and was the subject of carved netsuke up to the late nineteenth century.

These figures were more often in ivory than wood, since it was considered more Chinese and 'scholarly' in taste. Ivory had until the seventeenth century played little part in Japanese culture, being restricted largely to plectra and decorative inlay for stringed instruments, rollers for scroll paintings, lids for tea-jars and personal seals.

As the cover of this book shows, seals could be used in the same way as a netsuke. It is from a painted album of personal accroutrements and possessions made into decorative patterns and datable to around 1625, before the full policy of seclusion had come into force. Here two different *sagemono* – 'things to hang' (from the sash) – a brocade purse and a lacquered *inrō* – are attached to a gilt seal by a group of interlocking ivory rings. There is also a small ivory gourd-shaped object which may be an early netsuke, for small natural gourds and shells were used as such many centuries earlier; or it may be a container with a removable top for a drug or other useful powder.

Seals, used to imprint the owner's name in red seal-paste, tended to take

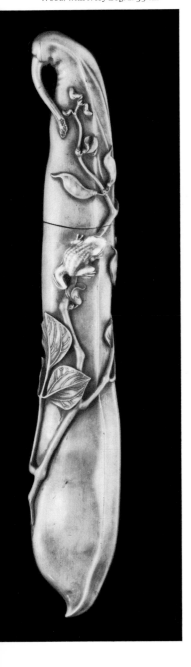

49. Knife-case in the shape of a bean entwined with leaves and a frog, by Kaigyokusai (1813–92). Wood, with ivory frog. L. 35 cm.

the place of a signature as used in Europe at the time and were themselves carved in wood, ivory, metal or hardstone quite apart from any decoration to the handle. They are the only objects in Japanese culture of the Edo period where the ancient skill of hardstone carving was maintained. The methods of carving the characters in relief or in reserve was closely related to the way catalpa or cherry-wood blocks were carved for printing throughout the period. It is worth remembering that seals and printing (as well as printing blocks for textiles) must have kept many thousands of skilled craftsmen in the art of carving in employment.

Decorated seals (50) were only one type of carved netsuke, though they seem to have been produced in far greater numbers than their representation in collections would suggest. There were also *sashi* netsuke (51) which were simply hung over the sash with the cords of the *sagemono* tied through or round them. Most, however, had two holes for the cords, and the tall figures of the mid-eighteenth century soon began to give way to smaller, more compact carvings, which made up in comfort, novelty and ingenuity for what they lacked in continental elegance.

By the late eighteenth century there were hundreds, if not thousands, of netsuke carvers, both in ivory and wood which was more to native Japanese taste. They made their netsuke to represent every sort of creature, plant or object. Animals, birds and fish became the most popular

50. (*Right*) Netsuke in the form of a seal surmounted by a tortoise, by Garaku. Ivory. Late 18th century. L. 3 cm.

51. (*Opposite*) *Sashi* netsuke in the form of a sea-dragon. Ivory. Late 18th century. H. 7.6 cm.

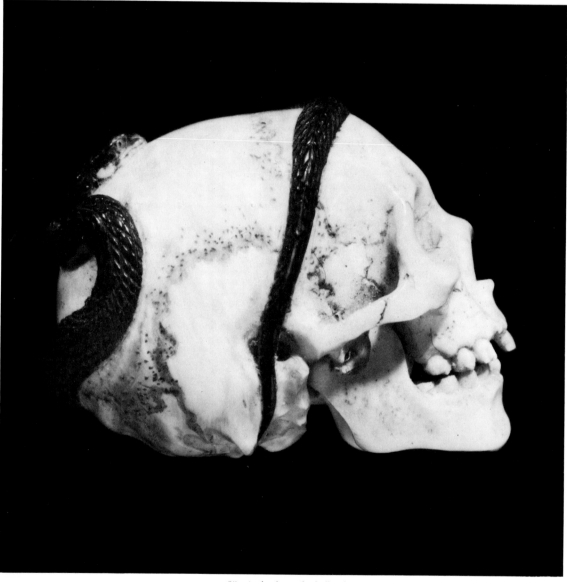

52. *Ojime* in the shape of a skull and
snake, by Sessai (*c.* 1820–*c.* 1880).
Ivory and wood. L. 2.2 cm.
(*Above* Reproduced actual size.)

sort, especially those of the zodiac animals which gave their names to each year in a continuously revolving cycle of twelve. They were, in order, rat, ox, tiger, hare, dragon, snake, horse, sheep or goat, monkey, cock, dog and boar. Colour illustration 3 shows three examples. One of a monkey and catfish shows the boxwood deeply patinated with age and use in the same way that European furniture matures. This is from the later eighteenth century and is unsigned. The single monkey is from the mid-nineteenth century and is signed Kōichi, a specialist in apes, the lines of its carefully engraved hairs darkening the wood with engrained grime, which cannot be safely removed by cleaning. The Chinese boy holding a young goat is in ivory, partly lacquered a deep coral red – a practice typical of the period after 1850 – and is signed Mitsumasa.

Neither of these makers is otherwise identified; they and the unsigned piece have been chosen as representatives of the very many unknown makers of the eighteenth and nineteenth centuries. Although many Western books have been devoted to studying named makers and their schools, it will never be possible to be certain about the makers of most netsuke because they were in many cases side-products of other sorts of carving, and these other products deserve far more attention than they have up to now received. The best documented example of this broad field of carving is that of Minkō (1735–1816), who worked in Tsu. He headed a studio, patronised by the local *daimyō*, and made small Buddhist shrines, sword-fittings (exactly what is as yet unidentified), temple figures, pipes, *suzuribako*, incense boxes and tobacco pouches. His netsuke were certainly not his major product; but after he became famous throughout Japan by way of publicity in *Sōken Kishō* (see p. 69) as a netsuke maker, copies by his studio, particularly of his celebrated tigers, began to be produced in large numbers.

Some of these other forms we have seen, as well as masks, woodblocks and seals, and transom panels known as *ramma* (3). Even more of a by-product were the *ojime*, or sliders, which held the two cords of a *sagemono* together. Two early ones can be seen on the cover of this book – one apparently in gilt metal and one either red lacquer or coral. The pipe-case and pouch (46) are joined by a carved wooden *ojime* with a Buddhist subject. *Ojime* were at their finest the most miniature of sculptural forms and had a special vogue from the mid-nineteenth century onwards when they were even admired by Westerners. Illustration 52 shows a remarkably fine example carved in the favourite *memento mori* subject of a skull, in ivory, with a snake, in wood, twined through it. It is by Sessai (c. 1820–80), who was well known for both skeletons and snakes and who has here combined his two specialities. It is hard to remember that the real object is only 22 mm long.

Netsuke carvers usually tended to make larger objects, and towards the end of the Edo period they began to make items with no particular function, marking an important shift in the way Japanese people regarded culture. Another snake piece, a carving in wood by Sukeyuki, done around 1880, shows this tendency: it resembles a netsuke but is in fact larger and too cumbersome to be used as such (54).

In the late nineteenth century these *okimono*, as they were called, were produced in gradually larger sizes and certainly in much greater numbers.

53. (*Left*) *Okimono* of a falconer. Ivory. Late 19th century. H. 42.5 cm.

54. (*Right*) *Okimono* carving of a rock, snake and fungus, by Sukeyuki. Wood. *c.* 1880. H. 9.5 cm.

The majority seem to have been sold to the West, where they stood as pure 'ornaments' to be admired for their astonishing technical virtuosity (53) and they were made almost always in ivory. It is a strange cultural twist that it is in ivory that the Japanese have come to be known as master carvers, a material for which as a nation they rarely had a deep feeling. A much truer example of their larger-scale carving is the beautifully patinated carp (55) by Mindō, a maker not elsewhere recorded. Surprisingly, it was made to suspend from a special wooden device; from the fish itself hung an iron kettle over a brazier. Such an object combines function and ornament in the best Japanese tradition.

55. (*Right*) Carp used as part of a *jizai* for hanging a kettle over a brazier, signed Mindō. Wood with ivory eyes. *c.* 1800. L. 44.2 cm.

4 LACQUER

Lacquer has for long been considered the most typically Japanese of materials, and although its use was developed first in China and South-East Asia long before the Christian era, the Japanese certainly gave it a very special place in their material culture from the eighth century onwards. Indeed, recent excavations have shown that it was known in the Japanese islands at a relatively early date, for both red and black pigmented lacquer coatings have been found on objects of the late Jōmon period (c. 1000–c. 250 BC), including bowls, vessels and items of personal adornment.

The use of lacquer ornamented in various ways as a decorative coating of very high quality for objects of all sorts was adopted from the civilisations of Korea and China and had become widely used in the palaces and great temples of Japan by the Nara period (AD 710–94). By the eleventh century it was being employed for the interior decoration of whole rooms and their furniture, often inlaid with mother-of-pearl or adorned with powdered or flaked gold. Thus Marco Polo in the thirteenth century, while resident at the court of Kublai Khan, first heard of the land of 'Zipangu' which was so rich that even the furniture was made of gold. At this period Japanese lacquers were apparently admired even in China.

When the first Portuguese visitors reached Japan in the mid-sixteenth century, it was the lacquer items which they recognised as being the most unusual and desirable objects for the Western market, and they were the first artistic objects from Japan to be brought back to Europe. The Portuguese, and a little later the English and the Dutch, ordered boxes and chests in Western shapes and some items for ecclesiastical use such as portable shrines and sacrament boxes. The gold decoration on black with some mother-of-pearl inlay which was Japan's special taste in lacquer became a standard for European ideas of Oriental design and had

56. Writing-box decorated with
autumn flowers and deer crying to
the moon. Black lacquer with gold
makie and metal studs. 17th century.
16.2 × 14.3 × 3.7 cm.

57. Portable picnic set containing a four-tiered food-box, trays and two wine bottles, decorated with floral scrolling in gold and silver *makie* over *nashiji*. 18th or 19th century. 23.6 × 37.1 × 32.2 cm.

widespread influence on furniture and interior decoration. We know that a large consignment reached London in 1614, including large chests, some of which are still found in great country houses. The very word 'Japanning' came to be used for lacquering, though European copies were made with shellac, a quite different substance from the sap of the lacquer tree of East and South-East Asia.

European visitors cannot have had far to look for lacquer wares, for by the sixteenth century they had ceased to be the preserve of those in positions of power and had become widely used by the ever-increasing numbers of the rich townsmen of Kyoto, Osaka and Sakai. Lacquer would have been seen everywhere in such places – on buildings, palanquins, as an outer coating to Buddhist images and altar goods, on furniture, writing-boxes, containers, food vessels, musical instruments, bowls, sword scabbards, helmets and even coating the metal or leather parts of warriors' armour. Because of its lightness it was much used for portable picnic-sets, boxes of games and the equipment of itinerant priests, such as the big framed back-packs containing images, scriptures and necessities of life.

All these uses for lacquer continued into the three centuries we are concerned with here, with the addition of export pieces (see p. 95) and small personal accoutrements, especially the little sets of interlocking cases called *inrō* ('seal baskets') which became increasingly popular as time passed and wealth increased. It was these exquisitely made small pieces above all which Westerners began to bring back in large numbers in the mid-nineteenth century when Japan came out of her Isolation. As a result lacquer, as well as metalwork and carving, has come to be considered a 'miniature' Japanese art.

The basic ingredient of lacquer is the sap of a tree indigenous to East and South-East Asia which is deciduous, buds in Japan in April and May, and flowers from May to June with thick sprays of yellow-white blossoms. The sap is bled from the tree between June and November, changing from a watery consistency at first to its finest during August, and later to a lower quality which can at least be used for making the *shitaji*, or underlayer of lacquered work. From the Nara period onwards there were extensive plantations of lacquer trees, especially near Kyoto, to supply the ever-increasing demand for it. Later cultivation moved to the north.

Into the sap, or lac, could be mixed colouring agents or fillers to prepare coatings which could be polished when dry to produce surfaces of lasting beauty. The earliest lacquered objects were coloured either black by using fine charcoal powder in suspension or vermilion by the addition of cinnabar, which is a mercuric compound, and these two colours have remained the standard ones for lacquer up to the present day. Other pigments were rarely used before the nineteenth century, except occasionally for yellow ochre which was the traditional pigment for layering with red (see pp. 83–4). The splendid decorative effects were produced rather by the use of gold and silver powders and flakes, by metallic, shell and other inlays, and by carving and engraving. These processes are described below.

Lacquer dries by means of an organic reaction between its constituents and requires the presence of water. Having dried, however, it forms a waterproof skin which can stand up even to boiling liquid, and hence is suitable for soup and food containers. If there is any flaw in the surface, however, or if the framework itself warps to produce cracks, then all these advantages are lost. While slowly drying, the tacky surface will easily pick up disfiguring particles, so extreme cleanliness in the workshop is essential. Thus the lacquerer needs a very clean and controlled humid environment in which to do his work. This is probably why lacquerers are so infrequently shown in illustrations, for they tended to hide themselves away in these carefully controlled workshops. The medical dangers of handling raw lacquer must also have contributed to the retiring nature of the craft.

Lacquer has to be dried in thin layers; each layer must be allowed to set hard and then polished before the next is applied. This takes a considerable time, especially on pieces which require a thickness in excess of 100 layers. Good wares, therefore, could never be anything but expensive.

The lacquer artist could usually start work on an object which had been built by a specialist maker. Metal objects, such as plate armour, needed little preparation, but most lacquering was done on a base of wood, leather, or other organic material. Wood had to be carefully seasoned and selected so that it would never warp and would retain the shape into which it was to be formed. It was most frequently used as it could be readily carved, bent, or joined to form the desired shape. Different types of wood were used according to the object being made – for example, cypress for boxes and fragrant magnolia (which exudes no resins or vapours harmful to steel) for the scabbards of swords. Bamboo plaited to form large basket-like containers was a common base for lacquer in the Ryūkyū Islands, which came under Japanese control in the seventeenth century. Leather of ox and wild boar was used since the Nara period. Softened in water and made to produce any shape, it was ideal for making pieces of armour, saddle pieces, bottles and other objects with curved surfaces. Early surviving examples are the lacquered leather travelling-chests in the Treasury of the Hōryūji temple in Nara, still retaining their shape after twelve centuries. Paper and textiles were used for light objects such as the flat, shallow dishes for drinking saké, or ceremonial court hats.

The next step in the process was the formation of the *shitaji*, or preparatory ground prior to the final layers of fine, polished lacquer, with or without the various decorative processes described below.

In Japan the most important way of decorating lacquerwork was *makie* (literally, 'sprinkled picture'), which was done by sprinkling gold (less often silver) filings or powder on to a tacky lacquer surface. The gold was sprinkled from a small bamboo quill, or *tsutsu*, over a thin layer of moist lacquer applied to the *shitaji*. When the lacquer set hard, the gold was retained in it giving the appearance of a matt metallic surface. In one form of decoration used until the seventeenth century the work stopped at this stage, but most of the work of the *makie-shi* ('makie artist'), as lacquerers were called, was more exacting and several more stages were used. The metallic layer might be burnished smooth and a layer of lacquer applied over it.

Gold powder became the convention for official lacquer during the Edo period, but silver could also be used. The powder was prepared by filing the metal between heavy blocks into flakes or fine dust as necessary. Depending on the type and distribution of the gold-dust in the lacquer, the artist could produce a variety of ground textures, some containing sparse patches of gold and some richly packed and polished smooth to give the appearance of solid gold. The latter is called *ikakeji* or *fundameji* and was used, for example, on the dowry sets presented to brides of the upper samurai class, or on the palanquins of the great *daimyō*.

One of the most delightful and most used effects achieved in *makie* was called *nashiji*, or 'pear ground'. Flakes of widely dispersed gold were sprinkled over moist lacquer and when this was dried a further layer of lacquer was applied to cover the gold completely. This process could be repeated a number of times so that the more deeply-set flakes showed duller and those nearer the surface brighter, the whole having the appearance of a starry night sky. When the top layer was dried and polished, the gold flakes became visible glinting beneath the surface of the transparent lacquer. Silver flakes could be used to give a similar effect, and as pure lacquer is slightly yellowish in colour they appear similar to gold; however, silver tarnishes even when immersed in lacquer, and early examples of this technique appear dull.

Nashiji was used widely from the sixteenth century onwards and is one of the most typically Japanese techniques. At first it was used in smaller areas to represent, for example, leaves on a plant, but in the seventeenth century it was found more and more as a dignified all-over surface in itself or as a background to areas of even more brilliant decoration. In the

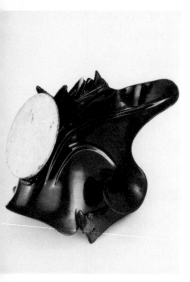

58. Helmet bowl suggesting a sea-conch, with the sun's disc as a *mon*. Black lacquer on iron. *c.* 1600. MAX. DIAM. 23.4 cm.

1 (Opposite) 19th-century *inrō: (top left)* with carp in gold and black lacquer and transparent lacquer over gold leaf. Signed Jōkasai. H. 7.8 cm; *(top right)* with carved cinnabar lacquer crayfish in high relief on gold *kirikane* ground. Signed Tōyō. H. 7.3 cm; *(bottom left)* cinnabar carved lacquer with plum boughs and blossoms. H. 8.5 cm; *(bottom right)* black lacquer with parakeet on leafy bough in mother-of-pearl and tinted lacquer inlays. H. 8.9 cm.

3 *(Above)* 19th-century netsuke: *(top)* Chinese boy with young goat, ivory with
lacquer staining. Signed Mitsumasa. H. 6.8 cm; *(bottom left)* monkey and catfish,
wood. H. 5.5 cm; *(bottom right)* monkey grooming itself, wood.
Signed Kōichi. H. 3.7 cm.

2 *(Opposite)* Box for the shell-matching game decorated with paintings of scenes
from the *Tale of Genji* in colours and gold leaf on paper over wood.
17th century. H. 35.6 cm.

4A (Above) Tsuba decorated with a cockerel confronting his image in a mirror, in high-relief
coloured metal overlays on iron. Inscribed Ishiguro Masatsune, but by a late
19th-century maker. H. 11 cm.

4B (Below) Pair of ornamental fittings in the form of a samurai with his retainer, and a lady with
her maid, in coloured metal inlays in repoussé copper. 19th century. H. 10.6 cm.

5 (Opposite) Storage jar with buff glaze enamelled with chrysanthemums and Tokugawa family
crests over a simulated brocade cloth. Mark, Bunka 2nd Year (1805), Tomonobu.
Satsuma ware, 19th century. H. 34 cm.

6 *Bugaku* mask of Ryō-Ō, the Dragon King, in brocade-lined box.
19th century. H., excluding movable chin-piece, 33.5 cm.

7A (Above) Lacquer comb box decorated with chrysanthemum blossoms
and leaves in yellow, green and black. 19th century. L. 17 cm.

7B (Below) Portable set of tea utensils including tea bowl, caddy,
bamboo whisk and blue and white paper-napkin holder. Different dates in
17th and 18th centuries, but lacquer container mid-18th century. L. 16 cm.

eighteenth and nineteenth centuries, however, its use as the surface for the insides of boxes became almost standardised, and many lacquered *inrō* have a *nashiji* surface inside their compartments. The gold particles tended to become smaller and more regularly sprinkled at this period, although they could be distributed in patterns, such as the clumps known as *gyōbu nashiji*. A form using rather large flakes which tended to lie flat instead of dancing in random array was called *hirameji*.

These processes were essentially intended to produce a rich gold or silver surface of more or less complexity; but naturally the makers often wished to add formal or informal patterns or pictorial designs to their objects and needed even more sophisticated techniques to achieve them.

The basic method of depiction was *hiramakie* (flat *makie*), which was done simply by shaking the gold powder over patches of moist lacquer applied to the surface of the workpiece with the shape of the intended design. This method is found particularly on work of the early seventeenth century, and especially on export pieces. The lacquer could be applied directly with a brush, as in free painting, and this was the case with most early work; but the design might be the work of an artist other than the lacquerer, who would provide a pattern drawing, or *shita-e*, to which the craftsman would work. In this case the design was traced on the back of the *shita-e* with a thin coat of lacquer and this in turn applied to the working surface by rubbing from the front of the *shita-e*. The gold powder could then be applied to the moist lacquer. The demand for ever-more naturalistic scenes to suit the taste of the later Edo period led to this method being used more and more and reached a climax in the work of the nineteenth-century artist/lacquerer Zeshin (p. 102).

Togidashi makie, or 'polished out' *makie*, was a method of producing designs perfectly level with the surrounding surface. First, repeated applications of layers of lacquer and gold-dust were made to build the design up above the ground. Next, layers of lacquer sufficient to cover the whole surface were applied. When these dried, the whole was polished flat until the design appeared through the covering layers. A very brilliant, metallic surface was produced in this way.

Takamakie (high *makie*) was the technique of modelling designs in high relief. Alternate layers of lacquer and gold powder were applied to build the design up above the surface. Charcoal, polishing powder and other fillers could be used with lacquer to form the bulk of the relief more quickly and cheaply. The raised areas could be sculpted and polished into three-dimensional pictures. This method was favoured for illustrating landscapes in which rocks, mountains and valleys could be formed with a three-dimensional effect. It was at its zenith in the late seventeenth century, when it was produced as a revival of the exquisitely detailed and lively lacquer of the Muromachi period, but the flavour was more naturalistic and detailed than in the early pieces, and a whole battery of other techniques, such as *togidashi*, metal studs, copper and lead inlay and combed effects to represent water, was brought into action to impress the rich townsmen from the great cities. From the point of view of technical skill these pieces of the late seventeenth century are perhaps the high point of Japanese lacquer art.

Inlays of other materials have already been mentioned, and they were a

8 *(Opposite)* Porcelain dish decorated with coloured enamels over underglaze blue depicting the poetical theme of maple leaves drifting on the Tatsuta river. Nabeshima-style ware, 19th century. DIAM. 20.4 cm.

81

major source of decoration in lacquer in the Momoyama and early Edo periods (*c.* 1550–1720). There were two important types of inlay – mother-of-pearl and metal – and these deserve some discussion.

The favourite inlay was mother-of-pearl (*raden*) which was the iridescent inner shell of various shellfish; from the seventeenth century onwards the *awabi* (abalone) was most used. The technique had been known since the Nara period, but it received a big impetus in Japan in the sixteenth century from the import of Korean lacquers which then very much favoured the simple contrast of white shell with black lacquer in bold patterns. These wares used large flat pieces of shell glued into depressions carved into lacquer, and the Japanese wares of the sixteenth and seventeenth centuries tended to follow this technique. It was most often employed on saddles and on the lacquered inner faces of iron stirrups, where the shell is frequently contrasted with a vermilion lacquer ground. There was, however, an increasing tendency to use it in combination with *makie* (59), and many of the earlier lacquers made for export to Europe were of this sort. The combination of gold, whitish mother-of-pearl and black lacquer has remained a typically Japanese taste, especially when the gold is used additionally to decorate over the shell.

However, mother-of-pearl was used in two other main ways: one was to raise it above the surface in relief, sometimes even carved or engraved (1);

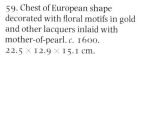

59. Chest of European shape decorated with floral motifs in gold and other lacquers inlaid with mother-of-pearl. *c.* 1600. 22.5 × 12.9 × 15.1 cm.

the other was the so-called Somada style, introduced in the seventeenth century in imitation of a quite different tradition, namely the Chinese one of inlaying into the lacquer designs made of tiny slivers of shell carefully selected for their green or red iridescence. Elaborate symmetrical designs or pictures of flowers, popular gods, animals or palaces were built up with great labour and patience on these pieces; the most commonly found are *inrō* and small boxes. This technique became the preserve of the Somada family by the early nineteenth century.

The Japanese fondness for contrasting one material with another led them to use metal inlay in lacquer at all periods from the eighth century onwards, but it was in the seventeenth century that the practice became most common. Wares based on the bold, broad designs of Hon'ami Kōetsu and the artistic school he founded with Tawaraya Sōtatsu favoured flat, shaped areas of metals such as copper, silver, pewter or lead set flush into the lacquer, a technique known as *hyōmon* ('surface device'). However, it was also common to raise metals above the surface in various relief effects. A problem with lead, which was particularly associated with the style of the painter Ogata Kōrin (1652–1716), whose designs were much used on lacquer, is that it often oxidises to a white powder which disfigures the piece. This, alone among Japanese metal effects, seems not to have been intended or foreseen. Smaller pieces or wires of gold or gilt metals set in lacquer were called *kirikane*, the same term used for slivers of gold leaf applied to Buddhist paintings.

The desire to reproduce that filigree-like effect seems also to have been behind the technique known as *chinkinbori* ('carved sunken gold'), which came from China by way of the Ryūkyū Islands in the late seventeenth century. It consisted of engraving fine lines into the dried lacquer and then filling them with a gold lacquer, which itself was polished down when dry. In this way much more delicately outlined designs could be introduced into a lacquer surface than ever before. Like Somada ware it tended to be used on small-scale pieces such as *inrō*.

There were, of course, many other materials which could be used as inlays – coral, pottery or porcelain, tortoise-shell, semi-precious stones and ivory amongst them. Most of these, as well as lacquer itself and metal and mother-of-pearl, were used at one time or another by Ogawa Ritsuō (1663–1747), who has been described as a lacquerer but was perhaps more of a maker of collages on lacquer or on plain wood carefully chosen for its beautiful grain.

There were other techniques of lacquer decoration, of which the most important was carving. In China vermilion lacquer, prepared with over 100 layers, which was then deeply carved into elaborate designs, had been produced since the fifteenth century. It was much admired in Japan and was made on a fairly small scale from the seventeenth century (1). Some of it came from the Ryūkyū Islands. Carved red (*tsuishū*) was traditionally popular, but a good deal of carved black (*tsuikoku*) was also made which was perhaps closer to the more sober Japanese taste. Also much to the Japanese liking was the process of lacquering in alternating layers of different colours

60. *Inrō* with chrysanthemums and bush clover by a fence. Somada-style inlay, in mother-of-pearl, gold *kirikane* and *hiramakie*. 19th century. H. 6.4 cm.

(generally combinations of black, red and yellow) and then cutting it back in arabesques to reveal the layers. This method, which was called *guri* and was much used on *inrō* for the more sophisticated townsmen, was based on the Chinese practice of cutting back red lacquer to reveal a yellow base.

Kamakura-bori was a short-cut form of carved lacquer which developed in the city of Kamakura in the late Middle Ages but which has continued up to the present day. The carving was done on the wooden base itself, which was then covered with far fewer layers of lacquer. Since this method was far less expensive in materials and time, larger pieces, such as low tables, serving trays, and large dishes and boxes, could be made.

The Japanese fondness for the effects of age is most of all seen in the Negoro lacquers, named from the Negoro Temple in Kii Province (modern Wakayama Prefecture). Here, reputedly since the fourteenth century, saké containers were made of heavy turned wood, first covered by black and then vermilion layers of lacquer. These bulbous bottles showed wear through rubbing over the years, and the black then began to appear in patches through the red. This much-loved effect was soon extended to boxes, soup bowls, carrying-chests and many other objects, and was apparently produced during the Edo period in centres far from Negoro. It was always a semi-folk lacquer, and since the Japanese folk-craft movement this century it has continued to be made by self-conscious craftsmen.

Apart from the basic red and black, and very rarely yellow and green, usually in carved wares, lacquers were almost never used as colours like paints. It was, in fact, very difficult to introduce other pigments which blended satisfactorily with a lacquer base, and their presence is an almost certain indication of nineteenth-century or an even later date. Only Zeshin (see p. 102) was able in the mid-nineteenth century to achieve harmonious results with a larger range of colours.

It should be helpful to describe the main types of object which were produced by lacquerers in the period under discussion. Much the most common were lidded boxes of many different sizes and shapes, for the box was the basis of all storage in Japan. In case this should seem to be stating the obvious, it should be remembered that in Europe clothes, equipment, papers, utensils and vessels, armour, and many other things tended to be stored in a variety of different ways – they might be put away in cupboards or chests, hung on hooks, placed on shelves, or simply, in many cases, arranged on mantelpieces or the surfaces of furniture. Boxes played a fairly minor part.

In Japan, by contrast, few houses were big enough to include much cupboard space, and only the greatest houses had the luxury of a store (*kura*) in the grounds. Nothing was permanently hung on walls, there

61. *Inrō* with matching *ojime* and *manjū* netsuke decorated in *guri* style. Carved alternating layers of red, yellow and black lacquer. 19th century. H. 7.1 cm.

84

were no bookshelves or other shelves (except in kitchens), and there was nothing approaching large-scale furniture. As a result, most things were put away in boxes, many of which were kept in the space under the movable matting units of the floor. It is perhaps a mistake to think that a Japanese room was always austere and bare in appearance, as a glance at Illustration 7 will show. However, most of the objects crowding that rather grand room from one of the great Edo houses of courtesans would have been put away in boxes after use, including the sumptuous kimono and sashes themselves, the hairpins and ornaments, the books and paintings. On the table to the left can be seen a folding album of paintings placed on the lacquered box within which it would have been kept. Behind the older woman is an upright box containing sets of books.

Many of these boxes were made of plain paulownia wood, but for anything of value lacquer was frequently used. Prized Tea Ceremony

62. Vase for Shintō ritual. Negoro-style lacquer on wood. 17th century. H. 33.5 cm; MAX. DIAM. 24.5 cm; DIAM. of base 17.9 cm.

wares, for example, might be kept in a brocade bag placed in a lacquer box, which was then encased in an outer box of paulownia. Rolled paintings were treated in the same way. Colour illustration 7B shows a complete set of Tea Ceremony utensils (bowl, whisk and cover, caddy and paper-napkin holder) with a black and gold *makie* box specially shaped to hold them. Similarly, colour illustration 6 shows a mask for *Bugaku* (p. 62), itself partly lacquered, lying in its fitted lacquer box which is lined with gold brocade.

The need to economise on space was important, and boxes are often remarkably compact collections of smaller boxes. Cosmetic sets for women, for example, might contain many smaller pieces lacquered with the same design. They would contain face cosmetics which have changed very little since the Heian period: rouge (*beni*, made from the *beni* flower) for lips and cheeks; finely powdered rice-flour (*konuka*) to white the face;

charcoal black to paint in the eyebrows high on the forehead, the natural ones having been shaved off; and blackening for the teeth, which was continued in richer circles in the Edo period. Other boxes held the tweezers and brushes for applying the make-up and, of course, the long pins and short ornamental combs for the hair, also in many cases lacquered, especially in the nineteenth century. Sometimes all these would be kept in the small drawers under a lacquered mirror-stand, and the mirror itself would be kept in a fitted lacquer box.

Elaborate sets for games were stored in lacquer boxes in the same way. The most important were cards, the incense and shell games, backgammon, *go* and *shōgi*. Cards related to Portuguese card games introduced in the sixteenth century were popular, but it was the cards for the elegant matching games which were most likely to be kept in lacquered boxes. Such was the *uta-awase* game based on the classical anthology of 100 poems each by a different poet (*Hyakunin Isshū*). One set of 100 cards was inscribed with the poems, the other hand-painted with portraits of the poets. Since all educated Japanese knew the poems by heart, the matching cannot have been an arduous task. The shell game (*kai-awase*) was similar but with painted sea shells. By tradition, however, these were stored in a wooden box covered with painted paper (*2*).

If these were derived from the courtly past, then the incense game was even more the game for those with pretensions to elegance. It consisted in memorising the scents of different incenses burned at the beginning of the game, and then identifying them later and distinguishing them from others not already burned. A set included a score-board (often lacquered and with various and elaborate markers), score counters, cutting and preparing tools (with lacquered handles), a burner, the incense itself kept in painted paper wrappers, and a slotted and lacquered 'ballot box' for recording the written guesses of the players.

64. (*Right*) Lacquered nest of boxes for the incense game, decorated with the 'three friends of winter' (pine, plum and bamboo) and the Tokugawa *mon* in *makie* and *nashiji.* 18th or 19th century. 18.4 × 26.7 × 20.2 cm.

The game of *sugoroku*, very similar to backgammon, also had a board which might be lacquered but more often was of polished wood. So were the chequered boards for the strategy games of *go* and *shōgi*. *Go* has now become an international game; it consists of two players placing black and white counters alternately on the intersections of a grid of nineteen lines. The counters, though not lacquer themselves, were kept in often highly decorated lacquer boxes. The pieces for *shōgi* (Japanese chess) were similarly stored. Unlike modern chess, the pieces were all the same shape but of differing sizes.

Many of the lacquer boxes so far described contained smaller, fitted boxes inside. The *suzuribako*, or writing-box, was no exception. It was the essential possession of every person of education, in a society where the

65. Lacquer writing-box containing ink-cake, inkstone, water dropper, brushes and cutting instruments; lid decorated with a landscape in silver and gold *makie* on *nashiji*. 18th century. 20.8 × 21.7 × 4.5 cm.

written word had the highest possible prestige. It was usually oblong in shape, occasionally square, with a length of some 30 cm and a depth of a few centimetres. The inside was compartmented to hold the necessary equipment and was removable, either in its entirety or as separate parts. The most important piece of equipment was the inkstone, a smooth but abrasive oblong slab generally of dark stone, hollowed out to create a well where the water could lie. The surface sloped towards the well, and on that the ink-cake was rubbed down with a little water from a small dropper (usually of metal, ceramic or lacquer) to make the desired solution. The ink-cake, which was also oblong, was made from soot, derived from pine or vegetable oil, mixed with animal gum in a suspension and hardened in a mould. It might have moulded decorations or even applied gold-leaf designs and added scents; the finest cakes were often preserved unused.

Apart from these items, the writer needed brushes and a knife or a spiked instrument for cutting paper. These were kept in a long, lacquered tray between which and the inkstone might be the space for the ink-cake. The Japanese brush is recognisable by its structure. The hairs (goat was the best, but other animal hairs were used) were fitted into a cylindrical

stem of bamboo or wood, or sometimes porcelain, so that their diameter
was the same as that of the handle where held. This gave maximum
sensitivity between hand, wrist and brush. The brush was held at right
angles to the wrist, pointing vertically down to the paper or silk; by
varying the pressure a wide range of thicknesses of line could be achieved,
from the thinnest at the tip to the broadest at the stem. A Western brush,
as used in painting, bulges where the hairs join the handle and therefore
does not have quite the same flexibility.

There was normally no provision for paper in a writing-box. Papers
were kept in larger, flat, lidded boxes with bigger trays. These were usually
lacquered and highly decorated, as were the small reading-stands which
were shaped like very short lecterns, and the low writing-tables which

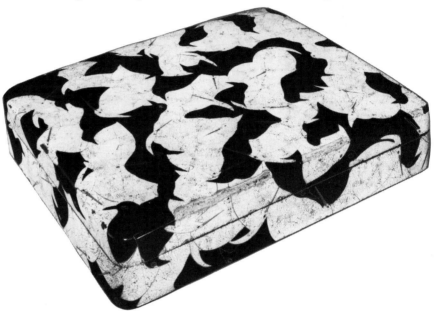

66. Document box with interlocking
crows and egrets. Black lacquer and
crackled eggshell-white, with eyes in
mother-of-pearl. Early 19th century.
30.5 × 24.3 × 6.2 cm.

were about 50 cm high and allowed a person kneeling before them to use
the brush vertically.

The finest decoration, however, was usually to be found on the writing-
boxes themselves, especially on the lid, which gave a clear space for an
unhampered design. Since the lid had to be removed to use the box, it
could be laid to one side and continue to be admired. For this reason the
designs are often very detailed, including landscapes of some complexity,
and this is true even in the sixteenth and seventeenth centuries when
design on other lacquer objects tended to be broader. An exception was
the style pioneered by Kōetsu and taken up later by Kōrin (p. 101). The
writing-boxes in this style were simple and powerful in design, and their
lids tended to be domed to give a three-dimensional cohesion lacking in
flatter examples.

Lacquered boxes can be divided into types according to the sort of lid
they used. A hinged top was never popular, and the rounded, hinged lids
found on chests made for export were a direct copy of Portuguese originals.
Now and again one may find a small box of games or cosmetics which
opens by sliding out a side or top panel; but the great majority of boxes had

67. Writing-box with pines against a rising moon. Black and brown lacquer, with silver and gold *makie* and copper sheet. 17th century. 24.1 × 27 × 4.2 cm.

either a lid which overlapped the sides or one which fitted closely on the top. If the former (7A), then there will usually be metal fittings for braids to tie the lid on securely. If the latter, the lid will generally fit so snugly on to its rim that no tying is necessary. This precision of craftsmanship encouraged the *jūbako*, or nest of boxes, which would fit on top of each other for ease of movement. They were much used for food, the close fit allowing each to act as a heat-retaining lid for the one below, only the top one needing its own lid. They are also found as part of portable picnic sets, held in lacquered carrying frames which also held saké bottles. Such sets would be carried to flower-viewing parties like the springtime visits to see the cherry blossom at Ueno in Edo; these might include a visit to the local shrine to the Tokugawa family.

By far the most common type of lacquered Japanese object found in Western collections is the *inrō* (1), the most miniature and precise example of the craft of fitting interlocking boxes together. The name *inrō* means 'seal-basket' and indicates its origin as a small container for the personal carved seal and sealing-paste which every literate person would carry (see p. 69). By the sixteenth century, however, it was also being used for carrying medicines or other small objects, or simply for adornment. The *inrō* was hung from the sash by cords, and that determined its size and shape. It would not be too large – the maximum length is about 12 cm –

90

68. Nest of food-boxes decorated with poppies in mother-of-pearl inlay and gold *hiramakie* on a black lacquer ground. Late 17th century. 26.6 × 20.7 × 23 cm.

and it had to lie flat on the hip. The most comfortable shape was therefore a flattened cylinder of ovoid cross-section, though a very shallow box-shape was also found. There had to be holes for threading the carrying cords, and the piece naturally had to be light and soft to the touch. A number of compartments was favoured to hold the seals and paste or to separate different drugs.

Given these needs, as well as the desire for *inrō* to be decorative, lacquer was the obvious material, and the skills in making interlocking boxes were used to produce the miracles of close-fitting precision produced in such large numbers between AD 1600 and the late nineteenth century. An *inrō* could consist of only one compartment with a lid, but most have three, four or five, and any number up to seven is possible. Not only did these have to fit perfectly together and yet pull apart with ease, but the two rows of holes which ran down the length of each side also had to be in very accurate alignment to thread the cords.

The inside of an *inrō* was often finished in *nashiji* – with very fine, small flecks of gold-leaf – but sometimes a plain red, brown or black finish is found. The outside provided a constant challenge to the inventiveness, ingenuity and skill of the decorative lacquer artist. By convention the design had to carry over the horizontal lines marking the compartment joints, which ideally should be invisible at a distance. It might extend all round the piece, or there might be different subjects on the two main faces. The maker, however, had more to contend with, for as *inrō* became more and more connoisseurs' pieces, and indeed it is recorded that they were being collected in Japan during the Edo period, they had to stand up to very close scrutiny. There must be no faltering in the line of the trunk of a tree or the stalk of a plant, even though the gold *makie*, incised groove, or inlaid mother-of-pearl or metal with which it was outlined was broken three or four times by the divisions of the compartments. *Inrō* in *guri* or carved lacquer were especially demanding for that reason.

Inrō could be made in other materials, especially wood, but they tended to be one-case pieces, either carved into a novel shape or with applied decoration in other materials such as metals. Some were carved completely out of ivory, but the shrinkage of the material over a long period causes the joints to loosen. Metal and ceramic examples exist but are heavy and impractical, made more as displays of technical skill than for use.

Inrō are sometimes found with the netsuke made to match, and even the *ojime* (*1*, bottom left). A netsuke itself consisting of a small lacquered box gave further opportunities to display the skills of the lacquerer of miniatures. Carved lacquer netsuke are quite common, almost always in red.

Apart from the box shapes, lacquer was extensively used on food receptacles on a base of turned or carved wood. The upper classes had used lacquered wares for the table since the Nara period, while the poor had used plain wood or pottery where available. Round wares included covered soup bowls, shallow dishes for fish or vegetables, larger, high-sided containers for rice, and saké bottles (*tokkuri*) which were tall and narrow so that they could be placed in hot water to warm the saké. These were also made over metal bases. None of these wares was the subject of much decoration, and plain black, or more commonly plain red, was favoured.

Musical instruments were often lacquered for strength, sound and decoration. Wind instruments such as the *yokobue*, or horizontal flute, and the *shō* (mouth-organ) had bamboo tubes partly lacquered to make them impervious to spittle. The bodies of hand-drums (*kozutsumi*), as used in *Nō*, *Kabuki* and *Bugaku* performances, were also lacquered, normally in black, and some gold *makie* decoration was used. The sound-boxes of stringed instruments were rarely lacquered, being preferably of grained and polished wood.

A completely different class of object to which lacquer was applied was arms and armour. Coatings of lacquer would protect metal from rust and other forms of corrosion, so it was often used on armour, helmets and the outsides of the scabbards of swords, spears and glaives. Indeed, a blade secured tightly in a lacquered wood scabbard by a closely fitting copper collar could be carried in the worst of conditions without a hint of moisture reaching the steel. The hard-wearing nature of lacquer made it yet more attractive to the military.

Sword scabbards were made in several forms of lacquer decoration. A plain, polished black was perhaps the most favoured, but many different forms of inlay and sunken decoration, with fine pieces of shell or metal set into lacquer polished smooth for ease of handling, were bought by samurai and civilian alike. The skin of the giant ray with the spines polished flat and clear-lacquered produced strong, lasting and attractive scabbards.

69. *Inrō* decorated with groves of trees in gold *makie* on a dark-brown lacquer ground. Signed Yoshimitsu. Late 18th century. H. 8.2 cm.

As protective coating for saddles, lacquer was normal because it was light and waterproof. While the seat, which would be covered by a piece of leather, might be plain or in simple *nashiji*, the front and back pieces were often richly decorated in *makie*, especially *takamakie*, or with designs inlaid in mother-of-pearl. The arched shape of these pieces provided a challenge to the designer and decorator which they accepted with enthusiasm.

Strangely, in view of this rich history of lacquered wares, the best-known Japanese lacquers in the West, not even excluding *inrō*, are the large cabinets which were exported in the last quarter of the nineteenth century. These are an adaptation of the European dresser and are usually elaborately inlaid with mother-of-pearl, and have applied plaques of ivory on panels of red or black lacquer with *makie* usually forming the background. These 'Japanese cabinets' are relatively common and they show how lacquerers, wood and ivory carvers adapted at that period from their traditional crafts to the new export fields opened to them by the end of the Isolation.

Lacquer had much continuity of function and place of manufacture during the period 1600–1900. Most of it was made in Kyoto and later in Edo, and the local varieties such as the Kamakura and Negoro styles did not have a major effect on central taste, although like most local products during the Edo period they did become increasingly known for themselves.

70. Saddle decorated outside with dragons among clouds in gold, silver and 'rust' *takamakie* lacquer; inside with patterns inlaid in mother-of-pearl. 17th century. L. 38.5 cm; H. 26.5 cm; w. 40.5 cm.

71. Travelling case for a sword decorated with a fruiting vine in mother-of-pearl, *makie* and *nashiji* on a black lacquer ground. 17th century. L. 112.5 cm.

Lacquer wares are therefore a good subject for a survey of the changes of style over those centuries, and of the reasons for those changes, which are, almost inevitably, social and economic.

The late sixteenth century saw a breaking down of established styles and an expansive mixing of many new types of decoration drawn from outside Japan. The effects of this in the arts continued up to the period of Isolation in the 1630s and less strongly but still with influence after it, although the Tokugawas had begun to discourage display right at the beginning of their rule. One element in this display was the use of subjects from ordinary urban life and a literal directness typical of the new rich, and these tendencies continued to conflict throughout the Edo period with the restraint demanded of the ruling samurai class. From the early seventeenth century onwards, however, the most thoughtfully artistic members of the urban class reacted against both and espoused the ancient aesthetic traditions of the Kyoto court, with whom they curiously identified as fellow-sufferers of the Tokugawa repression.

The above summary includes all the elements and forces which circled round each other and inter-reacted throughout the three centuries under discussion, ending after 1853 with a new and more massive influx of foreign influence and demand which was to produce the *Japonaiserie* wares which now swamp Western collections.

The export lacquers of the late sixteenth and first half of the seventeenth centuries were made mainly for Europe, and they can easily be recognised by their un-Japanese shapes (59). Their decorative style, too, is unlike that of any native taste, being crowded and rather incoherent. Typically it consists, especially up to about 1610, of cartouches or panels of birds on fruiting boughs (rather reminiscent of Mughal taste) or of traditional motifs such as wisteria, deer, maples, banded fences, pheasants and pines, and ceremonial wheeled vehicles, which were often somewhat confused with each other, as if the makers were using their least sophisticated craftsmen. These panels were done in simple *hiramakie*, with pieces of mother-of-pearl inlaid, and were often separated by bands of formal floral or geometric patterns in mother-of-pearl on a plain black lacquer ground (59).

The use of large pieces of mother-of-pearl is common at this period and was itself derived from copying Korean wares. The export wares after about 1610 used less of it and concentrated on *hiramakie* panels, sometimes very big, sometimes set in *nashiji* backgrounds. Naturally, pieces in specifically Christian shapes, such as host-boxes and miniature shrines, predate the suppression of the European religion, which was applied with increasing severity after 1614, and are in the earlier style.

A broad use of mother-of-pearl is common in native Japanese lacquers at this time but should not be confused with the very fine Somada inlay of later centuries (see p. 82). It is most often found on saddles, following a tradition dating back to the Kamakura period (70).

The export wares are themselves a reflection of the native scene at the time, in which the techniques tended similarly to *hiramakie* with mother-of-pearl and also to areas of *nashiji* used as part of the decorative repertoire rather than as a background. The style of the time was expansive, and these broad techniques served it. The favourite patterns were of flowers and grass – the 'grasses of autumn' (bush-clover, pinks, pampas-

95

grass and bell-flower are the commonest), bamboo, chrysanthemums and vines, the latter deriving directly from Korea and China. The plant motifs would sweep boldly across a piece, combining formal decoration and a sense of life in a way characteristic of the Momoyama style (71). Often arbitrary elements, such as *mon*, would be incorporated among them. Recently in the West this style has come to be called freely and erroneously the Kōdaiji style after the Kōdaiji Temple in Kyoto, built by Hideyoshi's wife, in which a number of celebrated and datable pieces have survived.

One of the most striking features of the design of this period, and one found on pieces from the Kōdaiji itself, is the slashing of the surface to be decorated into two quite arbitrary areas, each filled with a quite different motif. An interesting example is an *inrō* (72) associated by an old Japanese tradition with Hideyoshi himself. Here chrysanthemum blooms in raised black and gold (imitating stamped leather) spill over from the back on to the front in the form of a pouch fastening, cutting across a *hiramakie* scene of boats by the shore taken from medieval literature.

In reaction to this freedom an official style of lacquer came to prominence under Ieyasu and his successors. It was in fact a revival of the Kyoto style of the fifteenth and early sixteenth centuries in which pieces were covered in elaborate patterns or landscapes in gold and silver *makie*, combining *nashiji*, *hiramakie*, *takamakie*, *fundame*, gold and silver foil and even silver inlay in a surface of rich but restrained complexity. For this the very finest craftsmen were needed, and traditional families of makers, originating from Kyoto, were taken into service by the Tokugawa government at Edo. The most important were the Kōami; others were the Kajikawa and Koma, all of whose descendants continued working into the late nineteenth century.

The restrained ostentation of the official style was intended for the Tokugawas and their collaterals spread strategically about Japan, and for other samurai families of the upper levels. Sword scabbards for ceremonial occasions, for example, were decorated in this style, though quietly, but still in great contrast to the plain black required for ordinary occasions. The box for a *tsuba* decorated with two family *mon* in *takamakie* over fine *nashiji* is representative of the effect preferred (73). In the later seventeenth century, under the lacquer-loving Shogun Tsunayoshi (ruled 1680–1709), a peak of technical excellence was reached which extended for a few generations longer, though with an inevitable decline of invention and increase in surface prettiness. A typical example is the box for the incense game, incorporating the Tokugawa *mon* (which was used extensively by permission by remote connections of the family throughout Japan) in a rich pattern of pine, bamboo and plum blossom over *nashiji* (64).

Not all members of the ruling-class were able to afford such splendours, requiring months of work by skilled craftsmen, and as their economic position declined during the eighteenth century a simpler and rather duller type of ware was produced using a finely polished black lacquer background. Such pieces are the set of toilet equipment decorated mainly with the leaves and boughs of the paulownia tree (63) and the *shō* (see p. 92) decorated with the Tokugawa *mon* and floral scrolls known as *karakusa* ('Chinese grasses') which are often found on official lacquers (8).

72. *Inrō* decorated with chrysanthemums and a boating scene in black lacquer with gold *takamakie*. c. 1600. H. 8.9 cm.

The actual wealth of Japan increased overall during this period when the position of the warrior class was in decline, and it fell more and more into the hands of the merchant townsmen. This process had been going on since the beginning of the Edo period itself. It was not surprising, then, that those who had the wealth should have begun to patronise the makers of sumptuous and prestigious lacquers as well as many other products. The cover illustration is from an album of paintings of personal accoutrements of just such a man in the early seventeenth century, but interestingly the bolder and less detailed style of design of the Momoyama period can be seen on the *inrō* depicted there. However, the demand for rich gold *makie* was soon on the increase, much to the annoyance of the government, who in 1652 published an edict prohibiting townsmen from owning furniture and saddles of *makie*. In 1668 another prevented their owning *makie* articles at all.

73. Box for a *tsuba* decorated with arrow-flight and paulownia *mon* in gold *makie* over *nashiji*; woven silk lining. 18th century. 11.9 × 10.9 cm.

All the evidence points to these edicts' being effective for only a short period. However, the considerable increase in the production of fine *inrō* from the late seventeenth century onwards probably shows a prudent desire on the part of the townsmen to restrict their ostentation in lacquer wares to a small scale, easily hidden and not immediately noticeable when walking in the streets. Officially, makers such as Yamada Jōkasai of the Kajikawa family, who was active in the late seventeenth century, worked only for the Tokugawas; but his fondness for depicting animals does not seem in tune with official style, and a comparison with the system of work of the official Kanō painters suggests that there were ways and means of making money through highly unofficial channels.

Detailed literalness is a feature of this side of the taste of the eighteenth and nineteenth centuries, and the literalness tended to increase with time and to diverge further from the implied rules of restraint and use of space of the official style. Some *inrō*, especially those of the second half of the eighteenth century, show a charming fusion of the two, such as the sleeping boar with autumn grasses (74), the fresh and vigorous groves of trees (69), and the sea shells and weed imitating ink painting (75). Brilliant as they are, however, the *inrō* which strain after naturalistic effects in difficult materials are the last stage in this urban trivialisation of taste, as in the fish, lobster and cockatoo (1). Such brilliant technique and detailed naturalism found a ready market in the West after the end of the Isolation, and lacquerers turned their attention more and more to the latter-day pieces which fill many Western museums.

Interestingly, a further form of Westernised *Japonaiserie* grew up at this time, providing the customers with their own view of what Japan should look like. *Inrō* using scenes from *Ukiyoe* prints (76) are nearly always of the second half of the nineteenth century, and filled that need. Pieces showing ladies in heavy kimono with obtrusive hairpins, waving fans and looking at a distant mountain which more or less resembles Mount Fuji are likely to be even later. They are done in very thin *hiramakie*, thus reverting to a technical skimpiness and aesthetic confusion which was quite similar to what had happened three centuries earlier in export wares.

One must remember, however, that there was quite a different side to the culture of the townsmen, especially among the old families which had been rich since the very beginning of the Edo period, and that side is very apparent in lacquer wares. It is exemplified in the taste of Hon'ami Kōetsu

74. (*Above*) *Inrō* decorated with a sleeping boar and autumn flowers in gold *makie* on a black lacquer ground. Late 17th century. H. 8 cm.

75. (*Right*) *Inrō* decorated with sea shells in gold *fundame* and black *togidashi* lacquer imitating an ink painting by Mitsutada. Signed Kanshōsai. 19th century. H. 7.8 cm.

76. *Inrō* decorated with a courtesan in coloured lacquer and gold *makie* after a print by Eishi (1756–1829). Signed Shunshō. Late 19th century. H. 8.5 cm.

77. Writing-box with maple leaves
on a bridge over a swirling river.
Black lacquer with mother-of-pearl
inlay, gold *makie* and *nashiji*.
c. 1700. 22.5 × 23 × 4.5 cm.

(1558–1637), who came from a family of sword-appraisers, and whose name shows that his family had dedicated themselves to the Buddha Amida along with many other craftsmen in the Muromachi period. He was thus a *shokunin*, rather than a *chōnin*, and that may partly account for the favour he had with Ieyasu. As a designer he developed a style in lacquering which relied on simplicity of method and power of effect, and he may therefore be seen as a successor of the Momoyama style as well as of the more ancient courtly manner he professed.

Few lacquer pieces designed by Kōetsu survive, and none in Western collections, but there are a number of later seventeenth-century lacquers inspired by his example or by designs of his collaborator, the painter Tawaraya Sōtatsu. They are characterised by the very striking use of motifs, either reduced to simple outline forms, or seen in part or from an unusual point of view – the prow of a boat jutting diagonally across a bridge (78) or silhouettes of pines across an enormous moon, the latter inlaid in copper sheet (67). Such inlays of metal or mother-of-pearl in black or natural brown lacquer were very characteristic, and the use of *makie* was not pronounced. This may well have been one of the attractions to customers nervous of government edicts.

Themes from medieval literature, almost all of which was associated with the Kyoto court, were also favourites of this school. Irises blooming round a plankway over a pond, an ever-attractive visual theme, illustrated an episode from *The Tales of Ise*, while deer crying to the moon recalled many melancholy poems of autumn from the ancient poetry anthology of the *Manyōshū*. The late seventeenth-century box on this theme is one of a common type, partly inspired by Kōetsu and partly by the court lacquers of the Muromachi period, which too had inspired him (56).

Pieces like this show the gradual dissemination of the Kōetsu style into the lacquer of the seventeenth century, everywhere raising its standards of design. Exuberant pieces like the magnificent *jūbako* covered with poppies is just such a product of the Kōetsu tradition with the brilliant cheerfulness of the townspeople of the Genroku period. The poppies are only decorative, with no particular allusion, but their simplicity of execution in gold *makie* outline, *hiramakie* and mother-of-pearl is stunningly effective. They could almost be taken from a floral painted screen by the Inen studio, which carried on Sōtatsu's style until late in the century (68).

The great painter Ogata Kōrin (1652–1716), himself related to Kōetsu, brought the style finally out of the craft movement and into the contemporary urban world, and thereafter it was known as *Rimpa* ('the School of Rin', from the second syllable of his name). This lightness and elegance was just what the newly rich of Edo wanted, and it was in that metropolis that the Kyoto-born and -educated artist spent his last and most famous years.

The inkstone box (77), while not associated directly with his name, is clearly inspired by his poetic manner and is datable to the early eighteenth century. A simple footbridge, seen from almost directly above in the traditional *Yamatoe* manner, stands over a swirling river; on it are fallen maple-leaves. All these subjects would recall to the Japanese the transience and sadness of life. Kōrin's fusion of natural and unnatural effects is very apparent – the agitated rippling of the river contrasting with

78. *Inrō* with hares and a boat prow in brown and black lacquer with gold *takamakie* and mother-of-pearl inlay. 18th century. H. 7.8 cm.

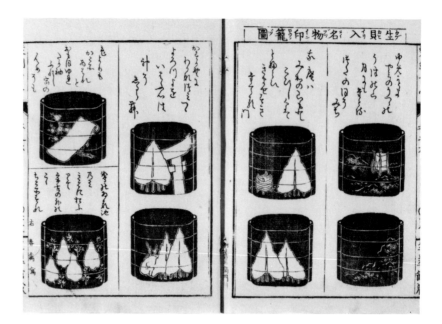

79. Examples of lacquered *inrō* with mother-of-pearl inlay from the woodblock book *Sōken Kishō* by Inaba Tsuryū, 1781. 285 × 440 mm.

the symbolically over-large leaves. The techniques, while not as austere as in the Kōetsu tradition, still avoid extensive use of gold; the background is in a very sparse *nashiji* which hints at starlight in the water, while the ripples are in painted lines of *hiramakie* tipped with silver for the ripples. Their delicacy provides another confrontation with the thick pieces of mother-of-pearl used for the bridgeposts. The bridge itself is in gold *hiramakie*, cut back into the black ground to represent the maples, and deliberately rubbed to give a feeling of age and that tactile quality so admired in Japanese taste of this sort. The piece is a remarkable example of how rich yet tasteful effects could be produced without exceeding the government's regulations.

Kōrin's style came to be debased in the later eighteenth century and was often reduced to a sort of visual shorthand in lacquer designs, the silhouette shapes being inlaid in mother-of-pearl or lead, the latter frequently oxidising to a powdery white with age. A page of such *inrō* designs in mother-of-pearl on black lacquer from the woodblock book *Sōken Kishō* (1781) shows how current this style was among the Osaka bourgeoisie at that late date. The method of silhouetting shapes such as fir-trees is not dissimilar to the hare in the *inrō* (78), in which the natural brown background lacquer and rubbed gold on the boat prow, added to the simple mother-of-pearl, give an appearance of antiquity which was no doubt much admired by the eighteenth- and nineteenth-century townsman. In such pieces the Kōetsu and Kōrin styles have been combined into a new tradition.

It is impossible to leave the subject of lacquer without reference to Shibata Zeshin (1807–91), who may be considered the most original of Japanese makers in this difficult material. Like Kōrin he was a painter but unlike him he was also a practical lacquerer. He began his long career as an artist, learning the fluid, naturalistic Shijō style from Suzuki Nanrei (1775–1849), and as a designer of book illustrations and prints. In fact, his *surimono* prints remained an important part of his work and income, and a similar use of varied striking design elements is found in both.

He studied *makie* techniques from Kansai II, the finest master of the old Koma family (1766–1831), but his innovations lay in the use of colour other than gold, and especially in imitations of metal patinas. One of his most delicate techniques was to imitate water by drawing a fine-toothed comb through half-dry lacquer (80). This design of stylised plovers over waves brings out his status as the true heir of Kōetsu and Kōrin.

The variety of his designs is greater than that of any other lacquerer; but, like every other great Japanese artist, he integrated tradition, contemporary movements and his own individuality. The even, crisp designs associated with his name could also be found in other lacquers of the first half of the nineteenth century. A fascinating example is the document box (66) in which the lid is composed of interlocking black crows (in lacquer) and white egrets (in crushed shell with mother-of-pearl eyes), the two as it were providing each other's silhouette and filling the entire surface. This piece, probably from the early nineteenth century, shows the fresh breezes blowing through Japanese design at that time, which were to awaken Zeshin and craftsmen in other materials as well.

His output in the last twenty years of his life has added a bewilderingly large body of work, from *inrō* and tobacco pouches to large trays and boxes, much of which found its way into Western collections. Almost inevitably it is technically superb but lacking the dynamism and sense of joy in the master's earlier work. His innovation of paintings in lacquer pigments on paper was especially admired outside Japan. They are usually small, but he was capable of larger compositions which, remarkably, could be mounted in hanging-scroll format without the cracking one would expect from rolling such thick pigments.

80. Food dish incised with plovers over waves in black lacquer against a grey sky. Signed Zeshin. Mid-19th century. DIAM. 9.8 cm.

5 CERAMICS

Pottery and porcelain have had a much longer and closer relationship with the culture of the West than any other Japanese art or craft. They had a profound influence on European decorative style in the two centuries 1650–1850, and since then on international style. Indeed, it would be impossible to consider contemporary ceramics at all without constant reference to Japan. This is all the more surprising in the light of the fact, which will have been readily understood by reading the general remarks in Chapter 1, that ceramics were never until recent years considered decorative objects within Japan itself.

The source of this original influence on Europe was the porcelain of the Arita district, which began to be exported by the Dutch at Nagasaki in the mid-seventeenth century; it was a substitute for Chinese porcelain, temporarily much less available in the disturbances which led to the change from the Ming to the Qing Dynasties. From that time onwards 'Old Japan', as it became known, slowly ousted the Japanese lacquer which had been in vogue for the previous two generations, and although after 1700 it was arriving in much smaller quantities, at no time did the supply entirely dry up. In the first half of the nineteenth century, indeed, it began to pick up again; and by the 1850s export-style porcelain, this time with decorated fine-bodied pottery as well, was pouring into Europe and North America to continue with only brief interruptions to the present day.

All of these wares were in some degree ornate and tended to be highly

81. (*Left*) Tea bowl with white brushed decoration under a black/brown glaze. Utsusugawa pottery, *c.* 1690. DIAM. 10.7 cm.

82. (*Right*) Dish decorated with a crayfish in iron-brown over a cream slip. Seto pottery, mid-19th century. DIAM. 25.5 cm.

83. (*Above*) Tea bowl with brown and black glazes, named 'Pine'. Raku pottery, 17th or 18th century. DIAM. 11 cm.

84. (*Above right*) Hexagonal pottery jar decorated with plum blossom in brown over cream slip, in the style of Kenzan and Kōrin. 18th century. H. 10.5 cm.

finished and usually symmetrical in shape in accordance with Western upper- and middle-class taste, although strangely none of these wares, or for that matter porcelain itself, was central to Japanese ceramic traditions. Native preference was for much simpler-looking pottery, falling into three main cultural types: (1) local pottery of the very disparate regions of the country, which came early in the twentieth century to be designated among the *mingei* or folk arts; (2) the wares, both local and metropolitan, made mainly for the Tea Ceremony; and (3) the art pottery of individuals such as Kōetsu, Kenzan and Mokubei, which was closer to the central urban taste of the Edo period.

Towards the end of the nineteenth century the Western art and craft movement became much more aware of these native preferences, and before long they had become Western preferences too, in strong reaction to the older, largely aristocratic taste which had led to the European *Chinoiserie* and *Japonaiserie* decorative styles (the two were frequently confused by their own creators). It would not be an exaggeration to say that modern international art pottery is dominated by this more austere side of Japanese ceramics.

While it is misleading to try to summarise the native tastes in pottery of a populous energetic nation over a period of three culturally eventful centuries, one can point to certain marked tendencies. There was little admiration for an exact, regular shape; rather the natural differences between pieces and the slight irregularities produced by the individual potter were considered to have greater charm. Fineness of body was rarely sought for its own sake; it was the sensuous feel of the piece and its special suitability for its job that received more attention. Following from that was a liking for a natural, earthy glaze, with the possibility of lively variation as the result of firing in the kiln. Often the shape and glaze were enough, but when there was decoration it tended to be very simple, in one contrasting colour or perhaps two or three very simply used as in the case of enamelled wares such as those of Kyoto (85). These tendencies can all be seen in a food dish (86) of Shinō ware, made in the early Edo period at one of the kilns which specialised in this type of Tea Ceremony pottery in the area of Tajimi and Toki in Mino Province (present-day Gifu Prefecture). It is on three low feet, with a turned-over lip and an irregularly squarish shape with rounded corners. The lip is decorated with very simple lines and circles, and the inside with a single stalk of reed, painted in a ferrous pigment which fired to a greyish-blue under the glaze. The glaze itself is a whitish-grey, naturally crackled and pitted, but an unglazed gap to the left has burned in the kiln to an earthy brown. The effects of Shinō were always unpredictable because of the lack of precise control in the simple, single-chambered kilns used to fire it.

Far from being considered crude, such a piece delighted the Tea Ceremony master with its variety, interest and close affinity to natural forms and colours. It would have been used for serving part of the light meal which sometimes accompanied the Tea Ceremony. The Shinō wares were named, long after his death, after Shinō Sōshin (1440–1522), a master of the connoisseurship of incense and of tea, though the precise connection is not established since the wares belong to the late sixteenth and early seventeenth centuries.

85. (*Above*) Saké ewer decorated with chrysanthemums in green and blue enamels over a crackled buff glaze. Kyoto pottery, 18th or 19th century. H. 16.3 cm.

86. (*Above right*) Food dish decorated with a reed in iron-blue over a creamy glaze. Shinō pottery, early 17th century. DIAM. 20 cm.

By the same process another type of pottery made in the same area was called Oribe after the tea master Furuta no Oribe (1545–1615) who patronised the wares of new, more controllable multi-chambered kilns which had been introduced following the new techniques developed on the western coast of Kyūshū. Illustration 87 shows another food dish of this ware, with its more regular but still far from perfect shape offset by a design combining symmetry with asymmetry which is thoroughly

87. Food dish decorated in green glaze, with motifs in white and brown over a pinkish body. Oribe pottery, early 17th century. DIAM. 18.5 cm.

Japanese in flavour. The inside of the dish is divided diagonally into two contrasting and unrelated sections of triangular shape: one is in a thick, runny green glaze; the other filled with a pattern of knotted braids in white slip, outlined with iron-brown, on a pinkish body which has been left to develop its own light glaze. This style is more the work of a self-conscious art potter, unidentified, as always with Oribe wares of the period, and the use of three added colours is unusually complicated on pottery (except for enamelled wares like those of Ninsei in Kyoto).

Two sides of the dish are decorated on the outside with motifs taken from homely-looking textile patterns, a practice common in Oribe wares and in many other ceramics. Simply striped and checked cottons were much appreciated by the tea masters and often chosen for the bags in which the prized tea wares were kept (88). A different sort of striped pattern can be seen on a seventeenth-century tea bowl of Yatsushiro ware, from a pottery-making centre founded by *émigré* Koreans in western Kyūshū. Here the chrysanthemum florets run between double stripes, as in a popular style of cotton cloth of the Edo period. Technically, however, this is a very different sort of piece, since the designs were stamped and engraved on to the body before it dried and filled in with a white clay slip, after which the object was covered with a grey glaze. This method, originating in Korea, was known as Mishima.

A related style, known as *hakeme*, was also much used in Kyūshū. Instead of incising and stamping, white slip was brushed on with a broad brush, and then the piece was glazed. Remarkably refined versions of this style were produced in the late seventeenth century at Utsusugawa near Nagasaki, with a thin, highly controlled wheel-turned body (by no means was all pottery done on a wheel) and a lustrous, blackish-brown glaze. In fact, so crisp are Utsusugawa wares that they seem to be imitating the effect of lacquer, though lacquer decoration never used free brushwork

88. (*Above*) Pottery tea-jar with brown glaze and ivory lid, 17th century, with brocade inner bay, polished wooden box and outer cotton bag added at various periods. H. of jar 7.5 cm.

89. (*Right*) Tea bowl with inlaid pottery in white slip under a greyish glaze. Yatsushiro pottery, 17th or 18th century. DIAM. 10.7 cm.

like *hakeme*. The example in Illustration 81 has been in the British Museum since 1753; previously it belonged to Sir Hans Sloane who probably bought it from the family of Engelbert Kaempfer, a German physician who was at the Dutch trading-post in Nagasaki in the early 1690s, when the Utsusugawa kiln was quite new.

It was most unusual for Europeans to bring back anything but the porcelains made specially to meet their taste at Arita, the main and, for a while, probably the only centre of porcelain production in Japan. At Arita hard-bodied white porcelain with some resemblance to the long-admired Chinese wares was first made at the end of the sixteenth century by Koreans who discovered there the necessary white clay. They also introduced the multi-chambered stepped kilns, set into the hillsides around the town, which could produce the high temperatures needed to bake porcelain.

For half a century this fledgling industry produced only simple porcelain left in the white or sparingly decorated in cobalt blue painted under the glaze. The production seems to have been mainly for local use, and the wares had no great claims to be inherently better than the pottery of the Karatsu area immediately to the north or the Takeo area to the east, both also started by Koreans. This porcelain style, in unobtrusive, almost country patterns, remained in use right into the twentieth century and has as much continuity as regional artefacts in other materials.

Such wares are usually in the small, unpretentious shapes used for ordinary eating and drinking in Japan, and are far from the self-conscious spirit of the Tea Ceremony or the technical refinement of export porcelain. They include small dishes (but rarely large plates), oil and sauce bottles, saké bottles and cups, tea bowls for green-leaf tea (which were much smaller than the bowls used in the Tea Ceremony), and noodle-cups. An interesting example is a cup for eating *soba* (buckwheat noodles served in a broth), decorated with an alternating stencilled pattern clearly derived from the printed indigo and white cottons used in the loose kimono for wear after bathing called *yukata* (90). A more refined piece (91) is a saké bottle which was made tall and thin so that it could be set in hot water to warm. This has a more elegant but still very sketchy pattern of falling maple-leaves, a motif which would immediately evoke autumn to every Japanese. Both pieces are nineteenth century, although they could be a century earlier, so traditional is their style.

The needs of the Dutch gave the Arita industry a much-needed boost and helped raise its technical standards, for the Europeans demanded much larger, whiter and more brilliantly decorated porcelains. The technical problems of throwing plates and vases, such as were never used in Japan, had to be overcome, and strange foreign shapes, such as the coffee-pot (92), copied from silver originals. The crowded underglaze blue decoration on this piece is characteristic of the garblements of Chinese porcelain patterns made by the artisans of Arita – in this case a farrago of peacocks, rocks and chrysanthemums. However, to the Dutch traders and their customers at home in western and central Europe the style seemed both exotic and genuine. The metal spout on this piece was added in Europe.

The Dutch soon began to demand coloured porcelains, which the

90. Cup for *soba* (noodles) decorated with stencilled patterns in underglaze blue. Arita porcelain, 19th century. H. 6.5 cm.

91. (*Above*) Saké bottle decorated with maple leaves in underglaze blue. Arita porcelain, 19th century. H. 24.8 cm.

92. (*Above right*) Coffee-pot in European shape, decorated with peacock, rocks and chrysanthemums in underglaze blue. Arita porcelain, late 17th century. H. 26.5 cm.

Chinese had been able to provide earlier in the century, and the makers of Arita developed in the period 1650–1700 several styles of enamelling which are nevertheless unique to Japan. It must be remembered that until then they had produced neither coloured porcelain nor pottery, so their quick and original mastery was a considerable achievement. Two of these styles – Imari and Kutani – like the underglaze blue mentioned above, had the effect of hiding the fairly low quality of the porcelain body. One has become known in the West as Imari from the name of the port to the north of Arita from which most of the porcelains were shipped by coaster to Nagasaki. In Japan all the ordinary porcelain of Arita was called Imari without distinction, but in Europe it now describes a style of decoration using underglaze blue with overglaze rust-red, gilt and less often with some green, black, purple or brown. The Imari style was much in demand in the great houses of Europe and it had a strong and lasting effect on European porcelain styles. In England the Worcester and Derby factories both copied it, the latter right up to the present day. Illustration 93 shows a covered cup for tea or chocolate, an adaptation of the covered soup-bowl native to Japan. The panels are standard Imari chrysanthemums in blue, gold and rust, but the ground is a less common chocolate-brown with gilt floral scrolling.

The Imari style represents one side of Japanese decorative taste – that for the crowded, eventful surface, full of colour and varied motifs, resembling the rich brocades and dyed textiles used by the townsmen of Edo, Osaka and Kyoto. It stands in absolute contrast to the regional folk styles and to the super-austerity of the Tea Style. The Japanese called Imari-style porcelains *nishikide* ('brocaded wares'). After their decline as an export ware, they continued with increasing popularity in Japan itself. By the early nineteenth century they were becoming prestigious table-ware in the restaurants of the great cities and were being produced in large numbers in more native shapes.

By a strange twist it was the hitherto rather austere pottery kilns, controlled by the Shimazu *daimyō*, which in the late eighteenth century converted the brocaded style into what is now known in Europe as Satsuma pottery. It used exclusively enamels and gold over a fine, buff glaze and ironically had largely replaced Imari porcelain as an export ware by 1860. Much of this Satsuma pottery, which can be found in very large quantities in Europe, unfortunately has gaudy and tasteless decoration which obscures the excellence of what could be produced. Colour illustration 5 shows a fine piece in native taste dated to 1804. It is a storage jar for leaf tea, cleverly imitating in enamels the brocade silk square which was tied to secure the lids of jars containing high-quality teas.

The Kutani style of decoration used a different palette of enamels – green, yellow, blue, purple and black – to cover the deficiencies of the body. This was a native porcelain style (94) which is thought to have been developed in the late seventeenth century at Kutani village in Kaga Province on the north-west coast of the main island of Honshū. It was Japan's second porcelain centre and must have learned much of its technique from Arita.

93. (*Above*) Teacup and lid for the European market, decorated in Imari-style enamels and underglaze blue on a chocolate ground. Arita porcelain, late 17th century. H. 8 cm.

94. (*Right*) Large dish decorated with Chinese scholars within formal borders in Kutani-style enamels. Kutani porcelain, probably early 19th century. DIAM. 35 cm.

95. Hexagonal potiche decorated in
Kakiemon-style enamels. Arita
porcelain, late 17th century.
H. 31.8 cm.

At the same period the Arita makers learned how to produce a really fine, white body, and this opened the way to three types of porcelain which used that whiteness for different purposes and which have given rise to the romanticised Western concept of Japan as a land of delicate porcelains. These are usually known as Kakiemon, Hirado and Nabeshima. The best known is what is now called Kakiemon (95, 96), although that name was not applied to it either in Japan or the West until the twentieth century. It refers to a much more spare and elegant enamelling, delicately applied over a pure white body, the colours dominated by red, green and blue. The red resembles that of a ripe persimmon; the Japanese word for that fruit – *kaki* – is said to have been adopted into the name Kakiemon used by a maker of the Sakaida family from Arita who is claimed to have invented the technique.

Kakiemon was much admired by the Dutch, and like Imari the style of decoration became extremely influential in Europe. Indeed, the first true porcelains made in Europe at Meissen in the early years of the eighteenth century were copies of the Kakiemon colours and designs. They were later copied at other European factories, notably Chelsea and Chantilly. Illustration 95 shows a typical potiche for a European mantelshelf in a thoroughly Western shape; but a figure of a *wakashū*, a young man-about-town (96), shows that there was also a demand for the exotically Oriental. This piece has been in England since before 1690, and until the 1960s it was considered to be a woman. The kimono extravagantly decorated in wisteria boughs in the typically bold style of the Genroku era (1689–1703) and, to Western eyes, the un-masculine posture understandably led to such a mistake, but the posture of the body is not in fact one which would have been used by a Japanese woman.

The fine white body, comparable to that of the very prestigious best Chinese porcelain, led to the gradual adoption by the very rich of porcelain as table-ware. Until then the rich had eaten off lacquer, and they continued largely to do so, but porcelain's status certainly increased. Evidence of this comes from the development of the styles known as Hirado and Nabeshima.

Both were patronised by the local *daimyō*, whose domains happened to meet just to the west of the town of Arita. Hirado refers to the very refined blue and white porcelains made largely at the village of Mikawachi near Arita, which was under the control of the Matsuura family *daimyō*. Their first kiln was on the island of Hirado, hence the name. The early wares, perhaps going back to the late seventeenth century, are not identified, but they probably resembled Kakiemon using only underglaze blue. Such a piece, though its precise place of manufacture in the porcelain district of Kyūshū is unestablished, is shown in Illustration 97 of a food serving-dish. It is exquisitely decorated on the sides in lotus scrolls derived from Chinese Imperial porcelains of the early Ming Dynasty and on the lid with the 'three friends of winter' – plum blossom, pine and bamboo – and a chrysanthemum knop. The lid design represents that use of blank space and off-centre motifs which is most characteristic of Japanese aristocratic decorative style.

Domain-wares were mainly for the use of the local lord and his family and for the presents he had to give to his peers and to the Tokugawas to

96. Figure of a young man decorated in Kakiemon-style enamels. Arita porcelain, third quarter of 17th century. H. 30.5 cm.

stay in favour and to show that his domain was industrious and imaginatively administered to increase the general wealth. By the mid-nineteenth century the Hirado wares were being produced in quantity and sold all over Japan; they were soon to become a major export, and in the late nineteenth century Western houses were frequently filled with them, although by then they were being made in extravagant shapes using

97. Food serving-dish decorated in underglaze blue with 'the three friends of winter'. Arita or Mikawachi porcelain, 18th century. DIAM. 19 cm.

technique for its own sake to excite admiration. A more native piece from the mid-nineteenth century is the small teapot (98) decorated with the traditional Hirado subject of Chinese boys at play (often they are shown with peonies and pine-trees). This is the true Japanese pot for green-leaf tea, with a tube handle projecting from the side. The Arita craftsmen, however, did produce the Western shape of teapot, also for export, based on Chinese prototypes. In the Tea Ceremony there was no pot, the powdered tea being mixed directly in the tea bowl.

The Nabeshima wares were named after the *daimyō* family who controlled Arita itself. They established special kilns at Okawachi, isolated in the country to the north of the town, where their own private porcelains were made. The potters and their methods were jealously guarded, not against the near-by Arita makers themselves, who could be controlled, but to prevent the secrets of these special and prestigious wares from being discovered by other domains.

The Nabeshima porcelains were mainly dishes for serving food, often in matching sets of five and usually on a high foot decorated with a comb-tooth pattern in underglaze blue. The high foot emphasised the ceremonial and presentation aspect of the pieces, for in Japanese culture such a shape had the meaning of respect to the receiver. They were not export pieces, and few came to Europe before the late nineteenth century. With the end of the domain system in the 1870s the Okawachi potters and decorators came to Arita, and the style then became part of the general currency of Japanese porcelain design and excellent wares in the old manner were made there with enthusiasm.

For this reason the dating of Nabeshima is difficult. It is said to have begun in the late seventeenth century, and its decorative style supports this, for most of the designs can be shown to derive from pattern-books of

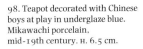

98. Teapot decorated with Chinese boys at play in underglaze blue. Mikawachi porcelain, mid-19th century. H. 6.5 cm.

the late seventeenth and early eighteenth centuries, especially those of kimono fashions current in Kyoto at that time. After that the repertory remained fixed, and few pieces can be confidently assigned even to the pre-Meiji period. What is not in doubt is that the wares represent much that is best in the cheerful, bold and yet tasteful style of the mid-Edo period; they are the most Japanese of all the porcelains.

Colour illustration 8 shows a thoroughly typical piece, using space with confident boldness, contrasted with glowing colour and intriguing juxtaposition of design motifs. The subject is a poetic one – the maple leaves of late autumn falling upon the turbid currents of the Tatsuta River, a theme evoking the transience of life but re-interpreted with a glamour which places it in its expansive period. These pieces were made by stencilling the underglaze blue patterns and then painting in the enamels by hand after the first firing. They were then fired at a much lower temperature to set the colours. Illustration 99 shows this painting going on in a page from the woodblock book *Sankai Meisan Zue* ('Pictures of Famous Products of Mountains and Sea', 1799); the scene is naturally not from Okawachi itself but from Arita.

In the late eighteenth century porcelain production spread to many parts of Japan, beginning with Kyoto, for over a century a centre of high-quality pottery with underglaze iron and blue decoration and overglaze enamels (85) and the home of the great art potters Nonomura Ninsei and Ogata Kenzan. This underlies the fact that, in spite of certain pockets seeking after refinement described above, the Japanese on the whole did

99. (*Above*) Painting porcelain at Arita, from the woodblock book *Sankai Meisan Zue*, 1799. 269 × 340 mm.

100. (*Opposite*) Saké bottle decorated with a grapevine in red and green enamels. Tosa porcelain, mid-19th century. H. 22.5 cm.

not make a firm distinction between pottery and porcelain. This was true, in general, of the Kutani wares (94). Indeed, there was in the Edo period a strong tendency *away* from the whiteness, thinness of body and regularity of shape of Chinese and European taste in porcelain, and what seems often a conscious attempt to make it look more like pottery and therefore more in harmony with Japanese material culture. Illustration 100 shows a porcelain saké bottle made in the mid-nineteenth century in Tosa province on Shikoku Island; it has a much closer affinity in taste to pottery than to porcelain. Its simple, clear design of grapevines is very close in spirit to a pottery fish-platter (82) made about the same time in the Seto district near Nagoya, and the two would not look out of place on the same table.

However, to return finally to a basic point made in this book, although most of the ceramics described here were in one way or another decorated, they were not, with few exceptions and apart from some porcelains destined for Europe, decorative. They all had a function, and without it their beauty in Japanese eyes was diminished. This profoundly native attitude had its most comprehensive expression in the Tea Ceremony, which has been frequently referred to, and a short description of its characteristics will complete this account.

The Tea Ceremony had its origins in Zen Buddhism, and its greatest master, Sen-no-Rikyū (1521–91), became a Zen priest. In his hands it partook of both religion and culture; but under his successor Furuta no Oribe (see p. 107) it became more or less secularised and remained so until the end of the nineteenth century, when it began to degenerate into little more than a social accomplishment taught to every schoolchild. Seen either way, however, it was not a ceremony, as the English word implies, but simply a meeting of people to drink powdered tea in circumstances of peaceful harmony with each other, with the objects used, and with nature itself. The Japanese name *Cha-no-yu* ('hot water for tea') mirrors its underlying lack of pretension.

By tradition and taste the pottery used was austere in the extreme and not in our sense decorated at all. Instead, glazes reminiscent of natural forms were much favoured. As a result of the power and patronage of the tea masters, certain types of pottery flourished producing wares which are very much more sophisticated than they at first seem. The most extreme examples are the flower-vases and water-jars of Iga (in present-day Mie Prefecture) which started as genuinely rustic and then became highly self-conscious, as a consequence of the approval of the tea master Kobori Enshū (1579–1647). Illustration 101 shows an Iga flower-vase which was made to hang in the alcove (*tokonoma*) of the tea-house and to hold a single, carefully chosen flower. It is crudely put together from gritty, unrefined clay, with deep, apparently random scorings down it. The glaze has the appearance of molten rock in green and brown, the result of slow firing over a period of more than a week. A very similar attitude and taste can be seen in Illustration 102 of a very hard pottery water-jar, made at the kilns in Bizen Province which gave the wares their name. Here the glaze is dark brown, with lighter flecks where it has failed in the firing.

From a water-jar the water would be poured into the kettle and then transferred in a bamboo ladle into the tea bowl, where it was mixed with the powdered tea. The tea itself came from a small caddy (88) and was transferred in a small bamboo scoop. The caddy too was of aesthetic importance, but it was the bowl that was at the centre of the Tea Ceremony, and hence of Japanese pottery. The most admired types of bowl were all extremely plain, whether they were from Karatsu or Agano in Kyūshū, Haji in the west of Honshū, Shigaraki near Kyoto, or of Shino or Oribe types from Mino in central Honshū.

Nevertheless, it was the so-called Raku bowls that held first place (83). These were made from the sixteenth century onwards in Kyoto, at first by the court potter Chōjirō who was greatly admired by Rikyū. Raku bowls were hand-made of light, porous clay with thick black, red or occasionally yellowish glazes, full of pits and blemishes. When they succeeded, they

101. Hanging flower-vase with green and brown glaze. Iga pottery, 17th or 18th century. H. 25 cm.

were considered the perfect ware for tea, soft to the touch and to the lips, holding in the heat of the tea, yet protecting the hands from it, harmonising visually with the dark green frothy liquid, and above all expressing the spiritual wholeness of the potter at the moment he made it. Seen in this context, the Raku tea bowl was far more than a pretty utensil; it was a symbol of a nation's aesthetics, and as such the best examples have always been the most revered of all Japanese ceramics.

102. *Mizusashi* (water-jar) for the Tea Ceremony, with ash glazes. Bizen pottery, 17th century. H. 15 cm.

6

POSTSCRIPT
TEXTILES AND THE HIDDEN ARTEFACTS OF JAPAN

Much reference has been made to textiles throughout this book, and so important were they and their patterns as influences on the other decorative arts that they cannot be ignored, although there are almost no good collections in the West to which reference can be made. Their flavour, however, can be understood from book illustrations, design books and the many objects on which they are represented or referred to. The Kakiemon porcelain figure (96), for example, gives a very good idea of the extremely bold style of kimono in the late seventeenth century, when it was common to fill the whole garment with one great motif – in this instance a wisteria bough irregularly laced with framed presentation plaques of the sort given to temples and shrines.

In contrast, the seventeenth-century gold silk brocade lining to the *Bugaku* mask box (6) shows a more formal type of pattern in which large flower heads are linked by stylised semi-arabesques of branches and foliage. Here the lotus, the ancient symbol of Buddhism, is used, but other plants could be treated in the same way, like the chrysanthemums on the lacquer box (7A).

Textile patterns were all-pervasive and found their way on to more ephemeral materials, such as decorated papers. Thus the stencilling of cottons which was a speciality of Osaka gave birth to an industry of stencilled picture books – *Saiga Shokunin Burui*, much used in this book to illustrate craftsmen, is a more refined version from Edo – and to the stencilled papers that are still produced in Japan. A roll of such paper, stencilled in purple and white with a minute regular pattern, has been

103. Purple and white stencilled decorative paper. *c.* 1690.

uniquely preserved in the British Museum since 1753, and probably came from Kaempfer (see p. 110). Similar designs were stencilled on to porcelain (103).

More elaborate papers, painted over gold leaf, were pasted over patterns raised in gesso and applied to decorative screens and to boxes, such as that used to hold shells for the shell game (2). The patterns, here of chrysanthemum heads and tortoise-shell scales, are again taken from textiles. Where gold-leaf was used, the designs tended to resemble the brilliant gold brocaded robes used in the *Nō* drama. The paintings on the box illustrate the eleventh-century courtly novel *The Tale of Genji* and would have reminded the owner, if indeed she needed reminding, of the medieval past which was the standard of elegance. A reading of that long work leaves one with a sense of the overwhelming importance in Japanese classical culture of writing, paper and textiles. They were virtually an obsession, and they always remained so, particularly since the lack of jewellery in Japanese life focused great attention on to the kimono itself. The size of the industry can be guessed from the late Edo print of a draper's department store (2).

The storage system described in Chapter 1 focused even more interest on textiles. Things of value were stored in plain paulownia wood boxes, or in lacquer boxes, but the object stored – for example, a tea-jar – would be kept in a brocade bag or wrapped in a square of silk, and the box itself might in turn have its own textile bag or wrapping (88). In addition, the silk braids used to tie up boxes were everywhere in demand in urban circles (9). Flat braids were also widely used in samurai armour to link

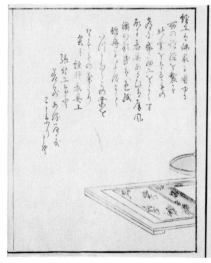

104. A mounter of scroll paintings from the stencilled book *Saiga Shokunin Burui* by Minkō, 1770. 285 × 380 mm.

the metal plates (14), and thick ones to secure court-mounted swords, saddles and stirrups. Wide braids were used to edge the *tatami* mats on the floors.

The mounting of hanging scrolls of painting or calligraphy further increased the attention paid to textiles, especially to the gold brocades and silk damasks made in the Nishijin district of Kyoto, for such paintings were usually edged in fine materials of this sort (104).

Variety was the keynote of Edo-period textiles and dress: cotton, silk, hemp and wool were the main materials, and almost every technique was explored – from plain dyed weaves to gold and silver thread brocades, woven silk damasks, fabrics dyed by wax-resist, tie-dying or stencilling, hand-painting, embroidery and patchwork. There was no dominant technique but rather a tendency to combine methods. Illustration 106 shows a silk summer kimono of the late Edo period, dyed in indigo with patterns of bamboo and cranes reserved in white by wax-resist. These white areas were then embellished with coloured embroidery and hand-painted lines in black.

As we have seen, the culture of Japan was based not only on textiles but also on other organic materials, and particularly wood and bamboo. One whole area of Japanese culture little explored from the Edo period is the

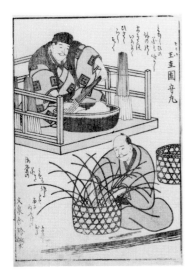

105. (*Above*) Waxing paper for umbrellas (*top*) and weaving bamboo baskets (*bottom*) from the woodblock book *Ryakuga Shokunin Zukushi* by Gakutei, 1826. 220 × 135 mm.

106. (*Above right*) Silk summer kimono, resist dyed on indigo, embroidered and hand-painted. First half of 19th century. L. 1.52 m.

remarkably elaborate weaving of bamboo strips into baskets (105) which were often signed by their makers. Another is the making of leather pouches, which achieved very high standards but which were little noticed because leather-workers were among those who were too despised to belong to a class. Yet another is the amazing range of fine papers produced all over the country. All of these, and many others, formed part of a complex and highly integrated material culture which it is not possible to understand without considering the role they played in it.

BIBLIOGRAPHY

JOHN ANDERSON, *Japanese Armour*, Arms and Armour
 Press, London, 1968

RICHARD BARKER AND LAWRENCE SMITH, *Netsuke: The
 Miniature Sculpture of Japan*, British Museum
 Publications, London, 1976

RAYMOND BUSHELL, *Collectors' Netsuke*,
 Walker/Weatherhill, New York/Tokyo, 1971
 The Inro Handbook, Weatherhill, Tokyo/New York,
 1979

C. J. DUNN, *Everyday Life in Traditional Japan*, Tuttle,
 Rutland, Vt., 1962

RYŌICHI FUJIOKA, *Shinō and Oribe Ceramics*,
 Kodansha/Shibundo, Tokyo/New York/San
 Francisco, 1977

TEIJI ITOH, *Traditional Domestic Architecture of Japan*,
 Weatherhill/Heibonsha, Tokyo, 1972

SOAME JENYNS, *Japanese Pottery*, Faber and Faber,
 London, 1971
 Japanese Porcelain, Faber and Faber, London, 1965

DONALD KEENE, *Nō: The Classical Theatre of Japan*,
 Kodansha, Tokyo/New York/San Francisco, 1966

KYOTARO NISHIKAWA, *Bugaku Masks*,
 Kodansha/Shibundo, Tokyo/New York/San
 Francisco, 1978

SEIROKU NOMA, *Japanese Costume and Textile Arts*,
 Weatherhill/Heibonsha, Tokyo, 1974

ROBERT TREAT PAINE AND ALEXANDER SOPER, *The Art and
 Architecture of Japan*, Penguin, London, 1955

BEATRIX VON RAGUÉ, *A History of Japanese Lacquerwork*,
 University of Toronto Press, 1976

BASIL ROBINSON, *The Arts of the Japanese Sword*, Faber
 and Faber, London, 1970

A. L. SADLER, *Cha-no-Yu: The Japanese Tea Ceremony*,
 Tuttle, Rutland, Vt., 1962

GEORGE SANSOM, *A History of Japan*, Dawson, Folkstone,
 1978

MASAHIKO SATŌ, *Kyoto Ceramics*,
 Weatherhill/Shibundo, New York/Tokyo, 1973

RICHARD STOREY, *The Way of the Samurai*, Orbis, London,
 1982

REIKICHI UEDA (adapted by R. Bushell), *The Netsuke
 Handbook of Ueda Reikichi*, Tuttle, Rutland, Vt., 1961

JAPANESE HISTORICAL PERIODS

Nara   710–794
Heian   794–1185
Kamakura   1185–1392
Muromachi   1392–1568
Momoyama   1568–1600
Edo   1600–1868
Meiji   1868–1912

INDEX OF JAPANESE TERMS

Page numbers in italic type refer to text illustrations; other references in italic are to colour plates.

aikuchi 40
ashi-kanamono 39
awabi 82

bashin 44
beni 85
Bugaku 58, 62, 92, 122;
    6 (colour)

chinkinbori 83
chōdo 15
chōnin 101
chonmage 35

daimyō 13, 19, 20, 28,
    32, 34, 35, 36, 42, 73,
    112, 114, 116
daisho 39

fuchi 39, 40, 43, 43; see
    also kashira
fundame 96, 98
fundameji 80
fusuma 10

geisha 9

geta 13
go 87, 88
guri 84, 84, 92
gyōbu 81

habaki 39
hakeme 109
hamon 33, 34, 34, 35,
    35, 36, 37, 44
hatamoto 19
hiramakie 81, 83, 86,
    91, 95, 96, 98, 101,
    102
hirameji 81
hiyato 32
Hōgan 52
Hōin 52
Hokkyō 52
hyōmon 83

iebori 42
iemoto 22
ikakeji 80
in 44
inrō 6, 23, 69, 78, 81,
    83, 84, 90, 91, 92, 93,
    94, 96, 96, 97, 98, 99,
    101, 102, 102, 103;
    1 (colour)
itame 33

jinie 34

jūbako 90, 101

Kabuki 92
kaeshizuno 39
kagami-buta 44
kai-awase 87
kamakura-bori 84
kami 21, 26, 55
kamishimo 35
kanamono 46
kane 34
karakusa 96
kashira 39, 43, 43;
    see also fuchi
katana 34, 39
kirikane 83, 83;
    1 (colour)
kōgai 39, 42, 44
kogatana 39
kōgei 9
kojiri 39
konuka 35, 85
koto 23
kotō 34
kozuka 42, 43, 44, 45
kozutsumi 92
kura 84
kurikata 39

machibori 40, 42, 43, 44
makie 77, 78, 80, 81,
    82, 85, 87, 88, 90, 92,

93, 94, 95, 96, 97, 97,
98, 99, 100, 101, 103
makie-shi 80
manjū 66, 84
masame 33, 35
meishoki 20
menuki 39, 40, 42, 44,
44, 46
minebari 21
mingei 106
minka 14
mokume 33
mon 26, 32, 35, 80, 87,
96, 97

naginata 34
namban 28, 40
nanako 41, 42, 43, 43
nashiji 78, 80, 81, 87,
88, 91, 94, 95, 95, 96,
97, 100, 102
nie 34, 34, 35, 35, 37
Niō 66, 66
nioi 34, 37
nishikide 112
Nō 1, 57, 58, 60, 61,
62, 63, 65, 66, 92, 124

obi 66
odō 25
odoshi 29
ojime 46, 68, 72, 73, 84,
92
okimono 73, 74, 75
ōyoroi 31

raden 82
ramma 17, 73

Rimpa 101
rōgin 38
rōnin 35

sagemono 69, 70, 73
sageo 39
sankin kōtai 19
sankō 14
sashi 70, 71
satetsu 28
semegane 39
Sennin 69
sentoku 25
shakudō 38, 39, 41, 42,
42, 43, 45, 46, 47, 49
shibuichi 38, 42, 45, 46
shinchū 25
Shinōkōshō 20
shinshintō 36, 38
shintō 34, 35
shirake 34
shirome 25
shishi 25, 42, 69
shita-e 81
shitaji 79, 80
shō 18, 92, 96
shōgi 87, 88
shōji 15, 17
shōjō 1, 61, 62
shokunin 9, 101
sudare 23
sugoroku 88
surimono 103
suzuribako 73, 88

tachi 34, 39
takamakie 81, 94, 94,
96, 96, 101

tanzaku 17
tatami 14, 14, 15, 23,
124
togidashi 81, 98
tokkuri 92
tokonoma 14, 17, 26,
120
tonoko 27
toran 36
tsuba 39, 40, 41, 42, 42,
43, 44, 96, 97;
4A (colour)
tsuikoku 83
tsuishū 83
tsuitate 15, 15
tsutsu 80

Ukiyoe 98
ujiko 34
uta-awase 87
utsuri 34

wakashū 114
wakizashi 34, 36, 39, 39
waribashi 44

Yamatoe 101
yari 34
yashiki 19
yo 44
yokobue 92
yosegi 57
yukata 110